D0920042

The Dynamic 1920s
in Europe and America

*Powerful Changes
Impact the 20ᵗʰ Century*

Arthur Drea

Copyright © 2014 by Arthur Drea

ISBN: 978-0-692-02-462-1

All rights reserved. No part of this book may be reproduced or transmitted in any form or by any means, electronic or mechanical, including photocopying, recording, or by any information storage and retrieval system, without permission in writing from the copyright owner.

This book was printed in the United States of America.

Cover photos: Lenin, F.S. Fitzgerald, Mussolini, Ataturk, Stresemann, Lloyd George, from Wikipedia public domain.

The design and layout of this book was provided by Mac-In-Town Graphic Design Services of Annapolis, Maryland. The typeface used for the cover title is ITC New Baskerville and the inside text is set in Warnock Pro, an Adobe Open Face typeface.

To order additional copies of this book, contact:
artdrea@comcast.net
410-573-0202

Acknowledgements

I am most grateful to my wonderful and highly professional editors, Kevin O'Sullivan and Robert Doyle, who did more than just edit, but provided many important substantive suggestions and error corrections. Although best efforts were taken to avoid error, to the extent to which there are errors, they are wholly mine. I am also grateful to the many individuals, students, colleagues, and friends, who offered kind words of encouragement throughout this endeavor.

As always, my deepest appreciation extends to my wife, Marilyn, without whose professional skills and fervent ideas this work could not have been completed.

Dedication

To Marilyn, my love and inspiration.

CONTENTS

Part 2. The Dynamic 1920s in Europe and the United States

The Dynamic 1920s
in Europe and the United States,
A Decade of Powerful Change

Preface

In doing research on the history of 20th century Europe, I have been impressed with the power of change that occurred in Europe and the United States during the decade of the 1920s. Certainly one could make a plausible case for virtually any period of time that resulted in significant changes in the environment and direction of a group of countries that then influenced the decades that followed. I make no argument that the ten years I have selected are either the most important in terms of future impact, or that subsequent events did not also have causal effects on the rest of the century. But often, important political difficulties have their origins in the past and require resolution in the future. I offer my proposition that the western world before 1920 (effectively before the Great War – 1914) was a vastly different world from that which emerged after 1930, and that the changes were irreversible.

For the United States the decade of the twenties offered a period of rapid growth and prosperity – a true evolution of a stable middle class. Americans experienced a mixed era of economic tranquility and carefree disregard of government imposed moral restrictions as the country went "dry" in the Prohibition decade.

In considering the many elements of influence that affect a country or region, both positively and negatively, I have chosen five important ones: 1) political stability; 2) rise of totalitarianism; 3) technical/industrial development; 4) military factors; and 5) science and culture. While this list is not meant to be exhaustive, it is broad enough to cover most all aspects that have had a profound impact on national development.

The countries I have selected to consider for the development of this proposition, in the order of their importance to the case, are the United States (US), the Union of Soviet Socialist Republics (USSR), Germany, Great Britain, Turkey, France, and Italy.

Any consideration of this decade must, of necessity, review the single most important event that preceded it, the guiding principles and decisions that culminated in the Treaty of Versailles. My research on this subject has relied heavily on the outstanding history of this Treaty written by Margaret MacMillan, *Paris 1919, Six Months that Changed the World.*

Annapolis, Maryland   Arthur Drea
April 2014
artdrea@comcast.net

Introduction

After the Armistice was declared on November 11, 1918, the guns were quiet but much remained to be resolved. In January of 1919 the heads of state of Great Britain, France, and the United States gathered in Paris to begin discussing how to remake the world. British Prime Minister David Lloyd George, France's Premier Georges Clemenceau, and US President Woodrow Wilson dominated the early conversations about a peace. Their views were very idealistic in believing that they had just experienced the "war to end all wars." They were guided by certain principles to which they nominally agreed. These are generally summarized as the Fourteen Points offered by President Wilson. Much of the conversation centered on retribution against Germany for starting the war unnecessarily, in the opinion of the Allies. The Germans, of course, did not believe they were responsible for the war and strongly resented the accusation. Nevertheless, the three principals discussed new borders, reinstatement of former countries, abolition of some colonies, consolidation of common language areas, and protection of minorities, among many other points. Both the British and French people had been told that Germany would be forced to pay for the war in territorial losses as well as huge reparations to be paid to Allied countries.

Because France had suffered the most and had a longer history of aggression from Germany, Clemenceau was the most adamant about weakening Germany in every conceivable way. Lloyd George was in a difficult political position because while his public comments and the sentiments of British citizens conformed to those of France, he was extremely concerned about the Russian revolution and believed that Germany was the only country that could serve as a barrier to the spread of communism. Wilson was also a strong anti-communist, but his overriding opinion was that "self determination," (a term he devised) by native peoples was the best safeguard against future wars. In addition, Wilson placed unrealistic hope in the proposed League of Nations to negotiate and settle all international disputes short of war.

To bring these three, and many other world leaders, together in agreement in the short time frame of six months that had been agreed upon, seemed to be virtually impossible. Of course, the Germans were excluded from all considerations of the Peace Treaty. As a practical matter, Germany had already relinquished all territory it had conquered since 1914 and specifically agreed to renounce all claims to Alsace-Lorraine. But the new government of Germany believed that many other issues such as colonies, national defense, and amounts of reparations were still open to discussion. They were to be shocked and gravely disappointed.

Permanent disarmament of Germany eliminated all warships except small coastal boats, and the standing army could not exceed 100,000 men. All warplanes, tanks, heavy artillery, and poison gas were prohibited. Reparations for starting an unjust war, a particularly sensitive issue, were set, after much discussion, at $5 billion each of the next five years and a final figure to be agreed upon for the next 30 years. Most of the German colonies were either eliminated or required to be shared with other European countries.

This one-sided Treaty satisfied very few in 1919, and it is literally true that the ink was not dry before efforts were underway, especially in the east and south, to change many of those decisions. Two national matters left unresolved by the talks in Paris were the movements of Russian Bolshevism and the breakup of the Ottoman Empire. Both developments are dealt with here in detail later but as of 1920 neither Russia nor Turkey was progressing as hoped for by the big three leaders.

The existent world powers at the beginning of the decade would be disappointed that the League of Nations would never really get started, especially after the US took nearly a year to ultimately reject membership. The universally accepted principle of protection of minority rights also was lost because no mechanism for enforcement, other than arbitration at the League, was proposed. Probably no mechanism could have been successful in any event, especially among the emerging nations.

One serious, but often not expressed, concern prior to the period of 1920 – 29, was the fear of the spread of communism. While Russia was still in turmoil at the beginning of the decade, it was becoming clear that Lenin and the Bolsheviks would prevail. A basic tenet of Marxism was that the revolution of the proletariat could not be limited by national boundaries but that it must and would spread. Some leaders, but not all, took this principle seriously as a true threat.

Thus, much was in motion at the opening of the third decade of the 20th century, and by the time the decade was over, many irreversible changes would make previous societies unrecognizable.

Chapter 1. Toward Disintegration (1895 – 1914)

European Imperialism

Imperialism is defined by *The Dictionary of Human Geography* as, "The creation and maintenance of unequal economic, cultural, and territorial relationships." The major European nations, during the latter part of the 19ᵗʰ century, desired to control lands that had raw materials needed for expansion and development of industrial economies. There was also a constant need to open up markets abroad for the goods that were produced at home. Nationalism fed the drive for empires – nations often felt that gaining colonies was a measure of their greatness. Christian missionaries added to the other reasons for overseas expansion because of a strongly held view that European rule would end the slave trade and convert many native peoples to Christianity.

As a result of these factors, many European countries began to seize lands in Africa. Technology helped them to succeed. Steam engines, railroads, and telegraphs made it possible to penetrate deep into Africa and still have contact with the home country. Sophisticated weaponry, especially machine guns, gave the occupying forces far greater power than any African people possessed.

The British Empire was the largest and most populous empire in the history of the world. It included colonies of various sizes and complexities on all the inhabited continents, and gave rise to the expression, "the sun never sets on the British Empire." The British colonies were very profitable primarily because of the importation of great quantities of natural resources not found in Great Britain and the fact that the native people supplied a huge quantity of very inexpensive labor. Even after World War I, Britain remained connected to most self-governing countries, such as Canada, Australia, New Zealand, and South Africa. However, the so-called "jewel of the crown" was India with a population of some 300 million and colonial profits that far exceeded any other British colony. In addition, during time of war the colonies supplied many troops, exceeding those from Britain itself, to the war effort of the Empire.

In India the British created restrictions aimed at preventing India's economy from operating on its own. Imposed policies and laws required India to produce raw materials for British manufacturing and then to buy back the finished goods from Britain exclusively. These industries included textile production, salt processing, and agricultural produce such as rice. Indeed the massive exportation of many agricultural products caused substantial famines in the late 1800s.

However, by the opening of the 20th century, Britain's policies toward India improved somewhat. Government officials were instructed to have a hands-off policy toward Indian religious and social customs in spite of the fact that religious missionaries were aggressively seeking to convert the native population to Christianity. Furthermore, improvements in local technology were evident; the world's third largest railroad network was in operation along with many dams, bridges and irrigation canals. Sanitation and public health improved and schools and colleges were founded. British troops cleared central India of bandits and put an end to warfare among competing local rulers.

France was also an early colonizer in the 19th century, concentrating on North Africa (present-day Algeria, Tunisia and Morocco), as well as central Africa (present-day Niger) and the island of Madagascar. The French were among the first to create colonies in Southeast Asia (present-day Viet Nam, Laos and Cambodia). The attitude of the French colonizers was more toward commercial exploitation and trade and less about political domination. Local leaders were used and accommodated more so than the British had done in India.

The Germans and Italians in the last part of the 19th century entered into the competition for colonies, mostly in north and eastern Africa. Germany had colonies in Africa that included portions of present-day Tanzania, Rwanda, Kenya, and Togo. Their principal Pacific island possessions were German New Guinea and German Samoa. German acquisition and expansion of colonies followed a plan and process with a minimum of friction with local leaders.

Mercantile domination was always the key as opposed to large-scale population expansion. Agreements were reached with other European nations, especially Great Britain, to share certain lands. However, only Togoland and German Samoa were profitable and self-sufficient. In spite of this, German leadership persisted in supplying and defending its colonial possessions.

Italian activities in the imperialist domain can be broken into two main parts. The first occurred during the "scramble for Africa" in the late 19th century and the early years of the 20th century. Italy, however, was at a substantial disadvantage to its European competitors because of a lack of financial strength. Only Eritrea and Somalia were acquired by the Italians during this period. Much later, in the 1930's, Mussolini was able to conquer and briefly hold Ethiopia, justifying in his mind a declaration on May 9, 1936 of an "Italian Empire."

Although there were tensions and disputes among the major European powers over African territory, the African war that caused the heaviest casualties and in many ways, marked the climax of imperialism on the Continent, was not fought by whites against blacks but among the whites themselves. This was the Boer War in South Africa. This part of Africa was comprised of several "republics" with substantial independence but connected loosely to a central government of South Africa. In the 1890s the Boers (indigenous population) began to be threatened by the influx of immigrants, mostly British, who were attracted by the discovery of diamonds and gold. Cecil Rhodes (who later established the Rhodes Scholarship) was the Prime Minister of the Republic of Cape and a heavy investor in African mining.

He attempted in 1895 to unite the Republics in sympathy with the British against the Boers. Rhodes was overthrown but the British pursued their interests and a full-blown war began in 1899. It was a brutal war with many casualties on both sides, but it eventually ended in 1902. The legacy of mistrust and bitterness between Boers and Britons lasted for generations afterward. By 1914 virtually all of Africa had been claimed by one European power or another. The possession of colonies became part of the definition of a great power and the competition for colonies helped bring on World War I.

However, that tragic war weakened the major European countries, and the growing nationalistic desires of the colonial peoples made it very difficult, and eventually impossible, to maintain control. Demands for independence resounded around Africa and Asia, but it was not until after World War II that these demands were realized.

Military Arms Race and Alliances

Germany became committed to a powerful military under the leadership of Otto von Bismarck, the most influential German Prime Minister of the 19th century, who had engineered the unification of the Prussian States. Because of concern about Russia, Bismarck organized a Triple Alliance between Germany, Italy and Austria-Hungary in 1882. However, he was relieved as Chancellor in 1890 by the young Kaiser Wilhelm II, who was very ambitious and impatient to drive Germany to military superiority over arch- rivals Russia, France, and especially Britain. The Kaiser already had the most powerful land army in Europe and wanted a navy to compare to the British navy, so he embarked on an unprecedented shipbuilding campaign after the turn of the century. Under Admiral Alfred Tirpitz the Imperial Naval Office began a long-term shipbuilding program with the goal of overtaking the British navy in terms of capital warships. In 1900 Germany passed a Navy Law, which increased the number of battleships from nine to twelve.

Britain had understood for centuries that its greatest security from foreign invasion lay with its sea power. The guiding principle was that to maintain naval superiority it would have to have a navy two and a half times larger than the next largest navy. In 1905 the British began construction of Dreadnaught (literally "fear nothing"), the largest and most powerful battleship ever produced at that time. Dreadnaught battleships were large, fast, heavily armored, and contained ten 12-inch guns. They were virtually impregnable, but of course other countries could also, over time, produce them. Thus, came about the very definition of a naval arms race.

The leading figure in Britain guiding this naval development was the First Sea Lord, Admiral John Fisher. It was under his direct management that Dreadnaught was built and many smaller cruisers were constructed. For political and economic reasons, however, Britain was anxious to substantially reduce naval armament building and end the race that the launching of Dreadnaught created. A proposal to that effect was sent to Germany in 1911 and responded to personally by Tirpitz: "Here is England, already more than four times as strong as Germany, in alliance with Japan, and probably so with France, and you, the colossus, come and ask Germany, the pigmy, to disarm. From the point of view of the public it is laughable...and we shall never agree to anything of the sort." After this unambiguous rebuff, Britain and France negotiated a secret naval alliance intended to buttress French naval security in the Baltic and Mediterranean Seas.

Germany kept pace and by 1911 had eleven Dreadnaught class battleships and Britain had eighteen. Similar arms development was going on with France and Italy with their land armies and weaponry. Germany widened and dredged the Kiel Canal from the Baltic to the North Sea to allow passage by its new, large battleships. Britain also built new naval bases for its capital ships, particularly at Scapa Flow in northern Scotland. This location was highly strategic because the German ships would need to go well north around Scotland to reach the Atlantic.

The French were greatly alarmed by this military activity in Germany, including a universal conscription, so they negotiated with Russia and in 1894 achieved the Franco-Russian Entente (an agreement of less force than a treaty between friendly nations). Britain later, in 1907, joined the Entente with France and Russia, creating the Triple Entente to counter the Triple Alliance of Germany, Italy and Austria-Hungary established years before by Bismarck.

Military war planning goes on constantly whether war seems imminent or not. So Germany had such a war plan for Western Europe called the Schlieffen Plan. General Alfred von Schlieffen was the undisputed military planner for Germany during the last years of the 19th and first years of the 20th centuries. He described his plan simply as, "The heart of France lies between Brussels and Paris." He developed a plan by 1906 calling for a massive ground force to move west through Belgium and then southwest to Paris. Other movements were essentially diversions in the south against French territory. The Schlieffen Plan remained unchallenged right up to the opening of hostilities in 1914.

Both the French and British were aware of the general aspects of the Schlieffen Plan but did not believe it would be politically possible to implement because Belgium was firmly neutral and its neutrality was guaranteed by both France and Britain. Invading Belgium would immediately widen the war. The French also believed that their long and well-fortified line of defenses on their eastern border would stop or greatly impede any German advance. Both assumptions proved false very quickly after hostilities began in August 1914.

East of Germany, Russia was viewed as vast and containing millions of potential soldiers but woefully unprepared. Worse still, the country had completely inept leadership on both the civil and military sides. Historian Barbara Tuchman describes Czar Nicholas II in strong terms: "The regime was ruled from the top by a sovereign who had but one idea of government-to preserve intact the absolute monarchy bequeathed to him by his father-and who, lacking the intellect, energy or training for his job, fell back on personal favorites, whim, simple mulishness and other devices of the empty-headed autocrat." French reliance on the Russians' delaying many German divisions in the east was not a widely shared opinion, and, as it turned out, France had misjudged badly.

So the alliances meant by some to prevent war, along with the arms race, were making war almost inevitable. The Kaiser and his ministers were very aggressive and bellicose in their communications and responses to proposals from the British for moratoria on arms buildup (as noted in the Tirpitz comments above). The Germans believed that the British were patronizing and simply wanted to maintain naval superiority at little expense. However, Wilhelm actually had made Germany's tactical situation far worse by alarming powerful and unfriendly nations to the east-Russia, and the west- France and Britain. A spark was all that was needed, but the actual spark was one that could not have been predicted by anyone.

Chapter 2. World War I and Its Immediate Aftermath

Minor Event Triggers Military Obligations

Many and various groups, especially in Eastern Europe, such as anarchists, nationalists, and communist revolutionaries, were organizing against the established order. In Serbia, which bordered Austria-Hungary to the south, there were especially strong feelings against Austria-Hungary because of the latter's domineering approach to its smaller neighbors and because of significant language differences.

When Archduke Ferdinand of Austria-Hungary, the heir to the empire's throne, visited Sarajevo, the capital of Bosnia and officially a part of Austria-Hungary, on June 28, 1914, he and his wife were assassinated by a young revolutionary who had been trained and equipped in Serbia. The Austria-Hungarian government quickly blamed Serbia. Although the Archduke was not popular in Austria because he had favored a republican form of government that would have raised the status of Slavs in Austria, he was, nevertheless, killed by someone who would have undoubtedly supported this policy had he known it. There are great ironies in precipitous violent actions.

As previously indicated, the Triple Alliance, created in 1882, consisted of Germany, Italy and Austria-Hungary. The Germans believed they were morally, if not legally, required to assist Austria in any international disputes. The Austrians were uncertain of German support, but their concern was not Serbia. It was Russian sympathy for Serbia. The Russians responded angrily to Austria's unreasonable demands, which amounted to loss of Serbia's independence, and the Austrian declaration of war on Serbia on July 28, 1914. There were strong Slavic relationships between Russia and Serbia as well as other ethnic and religious connections between them. The Russians partially mobilized their army near the Austrian-Russian border. On July 30th the Austrians ordered general mobilization of their military. (In the early 20th century mobilization of a country's military was often viewed as a declaration of war.)

The German General Staff had been concerned as far back as 1905 with the untapped military potential of the huge population of Russia. The leading

Army General, Helmut von Moltke, urged an early, decisive war with Russia while it was still weak and unprepared. Not all in the German government were in favor of war with Russia, but Wilhelm, who was still the final authority on these matters, was very close to and supported his General Staff. He viewed national treaty obligations as questions of honor for the country. In addition, German planning for military mobilization was very advanced and could be accomplished much faster than that of any other European nation. Germany also understood that France was not likely, in view of its obligations to Russia, to stand by and allow a quick defeat of Russia by Germany, thus establishing Germany and its ally Austria as the dominant force in continental Europe. Because of these reasons and his personal desire for grandeur, Wilhelm declared war on Russia on August 1, 1914.

The Schlieffen Plan, previously discussed, anticipated many of these situations involving the two front war. It prescribed the bulk of the German forces to first invade France, the more powerful of the two countries, while holding the Russians in the east to a stable or slowly advancing front. The Schlieffen Plan also envisioned invading France through Belgium, a neutral country, but Belgian neutrality had been guaranteed by both France and Britain some years before. The question for the Germans was would Britain enter a major war to defend Belgium or France? Germany's reliance on a military plan devised more than a decade earlier was one of the major miscalculations of the prewar period.

The Triple Entente at this time consisted of agreements of support between Russia, France and Britain. So by August 1st, Russia was faced with a major war with Germany and Austria. From the first days of the war, France was encouraging Russia to open a vigorous front in the east to relieve a major buildup of German divisions on the Belgian and French borders. The Russians promised a large offensive to begin by August 14, however they had made no preparations for such an early date and predictable problems of communications, transportation, and continuing supply developed immediately. Indeed, in 1914 the Russians had only 418 motorized transport vehicles and 320 airplanes, and few qualified pilots. Despite the Russians' initial successes with veteran troops in East Prussia and along the Austrian border, their supply problems became insurmountable and forced quick retreats.

By the end of July, the French military and much of the political leadership believed that war with Germany was imminent. German troops were assembled *en masse* at both the northern and southern borders between the two countries, and alarmingly, along the Belgian border. In addition to urging the Russians to take prompt and aggressive action, the French were pressuring the British to make it clear that they would enter the war against Germany if there was an invasion of France through Belgium.

The commanding French General was Joseph Jacques Joffre, who was demanding that his government authorize mobilization and movement of troops to the borders. On July 30th he told the leaders that if his demands were not met immediately the Germans would, "...enter France without firing a shot." Finally, at 4:00 pm on August 2, 1914, the French government authorized full mobilization and France prepared for all out war with Germany.

Even then the British were not willing to face what had become a *fait accompli*. There was a split among the British Cabinet, stemming from the Boer War, between the imperialists such as Prime Minister Henry Asquith, Foreign Secretary Edward Grey, and First Lord of the Admiralty Winston Churchill, and the isolationists who feared foreign entanglements. Most political leaders on both sides would not have supported a war simply to defend France, but the moral outrage of the threatened invasion of tiny Belgium was a more unifying cause. The first preliminary vote of the Cabinet on August 1st on the issue of an ultimatum to Germany against any encroachment into Belgium was a sound defeat of the proposition. Those who lost this initial decision were confident that Germany would very soon invade Belgium and thereby change the political calculus in the Cabinet. They were proved to be correct.

A week or so before, the British fleet had been conducting previously scheduled exercises in the North Sea and were due to disperse very soon. Churchill requested permission to keep the fleet and its personnel together, but he was denied. In a bold move, which suggested his later propensity for independent action, Churchill, with the secret approval of Foreign Secretary Grey, kept the fleet together and sent them to their war stations in Scapa Flow, Scotland. They were thus well prepared to resist any early movement by the German navy out to the North Sea.

On August 2nd, the French requested through diplomatic channels that the British respond to their concern that the German navy might appear in the Channel and threaten French ports. The British did respond that they would give all protection in their power to prevent this, but even this action would not require the British to declare war. Two days later the German army crossed the Belgian border and formally began the war. Later that evening, the British sent an ultimatum to Germany demanding removal of German forces from Belgium. Receiving no reply by midnight of the 4th, the British formally declared war on Germany.

Consequently, the creation of the Triple Alliance and the Triple Entente, meant by many to preserve the peace in Europe, actually resulted in a very sudden escalation involving five major powers. The greatest fear of Germany's Bismarck of a two front war was in fact realized. Germany faced Russia to the east and France and Britain to the west.

Allied vs. Axis Powers

The two sides now referred to as "Allied" (Britain, France and Russia) and "Axis" (Germany and Austria) were very well balanced militarily. The Axis powers, primarily Germany, had the strongest land forces and the best strategy. The Allied powers had greater financial strength, greater numbers, and the strongest naval forces, primarily British. The Italians chose not to be involved initially.

The Germans began their long planned offensive on August 4, 1914, by invading Belgium, and the "Great War" had begun. The Schlieffen Plan was followed at first but the Belgians did not cooperate – they resisted fiercely and slowed the German advance. The Kaiser was reportedly shocked that the Belgians did not roll over and accept German domination. Still by early September the German northern force was within sight of Paris. The opposing forces were generally separated by the River Marne to the northeast of Paris. The French fought a desperate, defensive battle to protect their beloved capital city and stopped the German advance. They even went so far as to requisition Parisian taxicabs and their drivers to ferry thousands of troops to the front.

The Anglo-French military leaders and their German opponents concentrated heavily on the Western Front, certain that the next time around, "with one more push," they could achieve a breakthrough. As a result, the lives of millions of men were sacrificed. Even on ordinary days, when the Western Front was mostly quiet, many soldiers died on reconnaissance missions and by shelling. Both sides launched gigantic offenses, but at best these gained a few useless miles. The trenches were protected by barbed wire and machine guns on both sides, thus producing a defensive war with little progress but much human sacrifice. Thereafter, the war in the west became the trench warfare for which World War I is most remembered.

During the next four years there were many large battles, but few of them had much impact on the ultimate outcome of the war, except for the massive loss of life on both sides. Although the Allies had greater losses than the Axis powers, the latter had fewer men to draw from. There are two battles that are worthy of mention because of their overall historical importance: the Battle of Gallipoli and the naval Battle of Jutland.

At the end of 1914 the war was not going well for the Allies and the proud British navy had had virtually no activity. Churchill, the First Lord of the Admiralty, devised a plan to attack the Dardanelles, the narrow opening between the Mediterranean Sea and the Sea of Marmora, which then opened to the Black Sea. The Turks had aligned themselves with the Germans and were providing harbor and safety to German warships in the Black Sea. If the British could capture the Dardanelles they could cut off this protection and supply the Russians in the north of the Black Sea. The land area protecting the Dardanelles is Gallipoli, a high position overlooking the narrows with Turkish gun positions facing the sea. Churchill convinced the Cabinet that Gallipoli could be taken with naval gunfire alone, without the need of ground troops. From February 19th to March 18th, 1915 five battleships, four British and one French, bombarded Gallipoli with long-range naval guns without discernable effect. Meanwhile the Turks had mined the narrows. After a long intensive bombardment on the 18th, the British tried to force the narrows. All the Allied ships hit mines and were either destroyed or severely damaged requiring them to withdraw.

There were further efforts to use ground forces, mostly *ANZAC* troops from Australia and New Zealand, but the Turks under the command of Mustafa Kemal repelled all efforts to capture the peninsula. Kemal was later named "Ataturk," the father of modern Turkey.

Jutland

Jutland is an area in the north of Denmark which faces west to a large expanse of the North Sea. By 1916, the German Navy had largely been bottled up, except for submarines, by the British Navy. The only way for the Germans to get to the Atlantic to attack British shipping was to go north past Denmark and around Scotland. This was hazardous because the British were vigilant to spot any German ships. The British fleet, known as the Grand Fleet, was stationed at three ports in Scotland, with Scapa Flow in the north being the main port. The British were under the overall command of Admiral John Jellicoe. The German fleet was known as the High Seas Fleet and was entirely stationed at Heligoland in the north of Germany. The Germans were commanded by Vice Admiral Reinhard Scheer. The two-day Battle of Jutland, on May 31 and June 1, 1916 was the largest and last great naval battle consisting primarily of surface ships firing heavy guns from great distances. (Of course, other significant naval battles occurred in World War II but those were dominated by aircraft carriers and airplanes.)

The Grand Fleet came down from Scotland in six rows of four battleships in each row, accompanied by battle cruisers, destroyers and other service ships. They were hunting for the High Seas Fleet which they had reliable information had left their home-port in large numbers. The High Seas Fleet nearly matched the British in Dreadnaught size battleships with 22 to the British 24. Early in the afternoon of May 31st, scouting parties from each side spotted the other and there were minor skirmishes, but it was not until 5:30 pm that the main bodies encountered each other, first by the faster battle cruisers and destroyers. But within an hour, the British had two battleships seriously damaged, one sunk, and the Germans had two destroyed. By nightfall the High Seas Fleet was attempting to escape the British by maneuvering behind them and then racing to the east. There were further distant encounters with light damage in the early morning hours of the 1st, but by 3:30 am the High Seas Fleet had reached the safety of Horns Reef in Denmark.

There were recriminations on both sides and, in the end the losses in capital ships and personnel were about equal, with the British losing somewhat more. The immediate result of the Battle of Jutland was the elimination of the German surface navy from the rest of the war. The long term historical lesson of the battle, which was not learned by most traditional naval planners for several decades, was the obsolescence of large surface gun platforms in later air dominated warfare.

The Russian Collapse in the East

The Russian Government, in looking back to the days of Napoleon, believed that the key to their military success was the mobilization of a huge army, which could then overwhelm any force attempting to invade. So in less than a year, the Russian army numbered nearly 10 million men, but they were woefully short of everything: officers, training facilities, weapons, food and virtually all necessities of an army in the field.

Throughout the war, it was common for an advancing army to supply only front line troops with rifles, with the following soldiers being required to pick up the weapons of those in front who had died. The condition of civilians was also desperate, with food and fuel shortages creating an ungovernable black market and complete disregard for any attempts by government to ration necessities. By 1917 human losses were staggering even by Russian standards. Over 650,000 had died and 2,500,000 were wounded in a hopeless war that few participants even understood. Constant labor unrest, added to virtual bankruptcy of the government and no reasonable leadership on the horizon, clearly offered opportunities to any revolutionary minded groups, of which there was no shortage. On March 15, 1917 the Tsar was forced to abdicate and a provisional Government was created which pledged to end the war on honorable terms. But it was far too late. Thousands of soldiers and whole units were streaming home to be greeted by famine and poverty. Discipline evaporated, and the war against Germany in the east simply ceased to exist.

Germany could not take full advantage of this collapse because it was also strained to the limit in fighting a two front war. However, important Russian industrial sites were seized. In March 1918, Germany offered what amounted to a surrender document (the Treaty of Brest-Litovsk) to the Bolshevik Government, then in control of St. Petersburg, and removed all but one million men from the eastern front to the west. With this new influx of men in the west, the Germans made impressive advances and by July were again at the Marne River, approximately 35 miles from Paris.

Although the United States had declared war on Germany in April of 1917, significant numbers of U.S. troops were not available in Europe until June of 1918. They immediately provided a decisive fresh force. The American Expeditionary Force, as it was called, was commanded by General John Pershing who made no friends among the Allied commanders when he refused to allow American soldiers to be commanded by anyone other than American officers. His view was that the British and French commanders had made a mess of the war up to that point.

The German advance into France the second time was quick, but its retreat was also very rapid. Allied and American counteroffensives were well-planned and German supplies and reserves were basically depleted. The German commander, General Erich Ludendorff, saw the inevitable collapse of the German fighting force, so he sought peace terms directed primarily at President Woodrow Wilson of the United States. This was a prudent move because Wilson and the US had not suffered nearly as much as the other Allied countries and would probably have been less vindictive in setting peace terms. Moreover, Wilson was known as an idealist who generally opposed war and had set out in writing his general principles to guide any post war discussions. The Allies agreed to an Armistice, which was not a surrender but a formal cease fire. It was agreed that the parties would return to the national boundaries that existed at the beginning of the war and that all fighting would cease at the eleventh hour of the eleventh day of the eleventh month in 1918.

Armistice and Paris Peace Conference

After the Armistice was declared on November 11, 1918, the guns were quiet but the worst military carnage in world history, even to this day, was far from over. The parties awaited a meeting planned for Paris in January of 1919. The chiefs of state of Great Britain, France, Italy and the United States gathered in Paris to begin discussing how to remake the world. Their views were very idealistic in believing that they had just experienced the "war to end all wars." They were guided by certain principles to which they nominally agreed, and these are generally summarized as the Fourteen Points, offered by President Wilson. British Prime Minister David Lloyd George and France's Premier Georges Clemenceau dominated the early conversations about a Peace Treaty, and much of that conversation centered around retribution against Germany for, in the opinion of the Allies, starting the war unnecessarily. The Germans, of course, did not believe they were responsible for the war and strongly resisted the accusation.

The three principals, Lloyd George, Clemenceau, and Wilson discussed new borders, reinstatement of former countries, abolition of some colonies, and consolidation of common language areas, among many other points. Although the original principal group included Vittorio Orlando of Italy, he was rather quickly sidelined by the other three because of Italy's relatively lesser role in the war and Orlando's complete fixation on Italy's demands to control Croatia and the northeastern portion of the Adriatic. The other three presented a significant contrast in personalities. Both the British and French people had been told that Germany would be forced to pay for the war in territorial losses as well as huge reparations to be paid to Allied countries. Consequently, this view represented the public positions of Clemenceau and Lloyd George.

Clemenceau was the oldest of the three and France had suffered the most of the three countries. Also, France had a longer history of aggression by Germany, so he was the most adamant about weakening Germany in every conceivable way. Lloyd George was in a difficult political position because while his public comments and the sentiments of British citizens conformed to those of France, he was extremely concerned about the Russian Revolution and believed that Germany was the only country that could serve as a barrier to the spread of communism. Wilson was also a strong anti-communist, but his overriding opinion was that "self determination," (a term he devised) by native peoples was the best safeguard against future wars. In addition, Wilson placed unrealistic hope in the proposed League of Nations to negotiate and settle all international disputes short of war.

To bring these three, and many other world leaders, together in the short time frame of six months that had been agreed upon, was virtually impossible. Of course, the Germans were excluded from all considerations of the Peace Treaty. As a practical matter, Germany had already relinquished all territory it had conquered since 1914 and specifically agreed to renounce all claims to Alsace-Lorraine. But the new government of Germany believed that many other issues such as colonies, national defense, and amounts of reparations were still open to discussion. They were to be shocked and gravely disappointed.

In June of 1919, a diplomatic note in unusually strong terms for diplomacy, expressed the outrage of the German Government: "Yielding to overpowering might, the government of the German Republic declares itself ready to accept and to sign the peace treaty imposed by the Allied and Associated governments. But in so doing, the government of <u>the German Republic in nowise abandons its conviction that these conditions of peace represent injustice without example</u>." (emphasis added). Here was an omen of things to come.

A summary of the Versailles Treaty is beyond the scope and purpose of this work but Germany's principal losses are important to consider, especially because they were used only a few years later to buttress the fascist regime of Adolf Hitler. As noted above, Germany relinquished all claims to Alsace-Lorraine, an area on the border with France that had about an equal number of German and French speaking citizens. Furthermore the border area west of the Rhine River in German territory was to maintain a 50 kilometer demilitarized zone. Permanent disarmament of Germany eliminated all warships except small coastal boats, and the standing army could not exceed 100,000 men. All warplanes, tanks, heavy artillery, and poison gas were prohibited. Reparations for starting an unjust war, a particularly sensitive issue, were set, after much discussion, at $5 billion each of the next five years and a final figure to be agreed upon for the next 30 years. Most of the German colonies were either eliminated or required to be shared with other European countries.

The two territorial pretexts Germany most relied upon in the 1930s to justify the beginning of World War II were the loss of the Czech-Slovak land in the east and the reestablishment of an independent Poland bordering East Prussia. Poland was also given access to the Baltic through the newly internationalized free city of

Danzig (present day Gdansk). All of these territories had been German at least since the days of Bismarck. The Germans believed, with some justification, that these lands had been well assimilated into the German Empire before World War I and were not causes of contention at the beginning of the war.

Chapter 3. Turkish Revolt

Mustafa Kemal Ataturk - Turkish Independence

It is not often that history can ascribe to one individual the credit for changing the direction of national, and even international, governments affecting millions of people, but such is the case with Mustafa Kemal Ataturk. (His given name was Mustafa Kemal, but the appellation "Ataturk," meaning Father of Turkey was given to him later by the Turkish people.) The relatively young military officer of the Ottoman Turks gained initial fame by leading the Turkish defense at Gallipoli in 1915 against the British assault to control the Dardanelles. But it was just after the war that Kemal began his most important activities to encourage the collapse of the Ottoman Empire and to create an independent and secular Turkey.

The once proud and powerful Ottoman Empire had been declining for more than a century, but the end of World War I was truly the death throes of what was left of the Empire. The collapse of the German offensive in July of 1918 and the destruction of large areas of Eastern Europe, formerly under the control of the Empire, added to the millions of deserters, made clear to the Ottoman leaders that the end of the Empire was at hand. Prior to the Peace Conference, some small hope was held that Woodrow Wilson would lead with a benevolent approach to existing nationalities and historic connections. But that last hope was dashed when, in January 1919, Wilson called for the Ottoman Empire to be dismembered and divided into sectors effectively under the control of the victors.

The Greeks, unlike the Ottomans, had chosen the right side in the war and were therefore aggressively asserting their claims to the eastern side of the Aegean and Mediterranean Seas, particularly the City of Smyrna (present day Izmir). Although the Turkish population was in the majority, the region was controlled by the Greek army after the war. The Greeks made a strong case to the big three in Paris that Smyrna was necessary economically and militarily to protect the Greek islands and eastern border of Greece from possible attacks by the more populous Turks. The British, French and American leaders listened almost exclusively to the Greeks, and in May 1919 they authorized the Greeks to occupy Smyrna and the coastal regions in far greater military numbers. The western leaders also feared that left-wing movements, including Bolshevism, would take a strong hold in areas of eastern Europe and that the Greeks were probably the best resistance to those movements. Indeed, there were communist sympathizers and many socialists in the remnants of the Ottoman government and all were seeking a powerful leader. But it is also fair to say that most of the Arab world saw three Christian men deciding arbitrarily, and in their own interests, the makeup and future of the Muslim world.

Mustafa Kemal was emerging after the war as a principal leader against partition of the Empire. He was one of the first to recognize that Allied diplomacy was completely at odds with the overwhelming Turkish opinion supporting independence. Kemal sought authority in the Imperial Government, nominally headed by the Sultan, and was given a military and civilian leadership position in Anatolia. He immediately began resistance activities against both the Greek occupation and the Imperial Government authority. When he was ordered to return to Istanbul, he refused and was discharged. Henceforth, he became a fully committed leader of a growing resistance movement.

The Turkish nationalists, as the resistance movement became popularly known, grew in numbers, and with the material and covert support of the French, became an effective military force under leaders who had gotten experience in the war. Kemal was their popular and undisputed commander.

As the military situation deteriorated for the Allies, a decision led by the British was made to allow the Greek army to move from coastal regions inland with the ultimate goal of occupying Constantinople. The nationalists melted back into the interior but remained organized. By August 1920, the Greeks had moved 250 miles into the interior. A counterattack the following month by the nationalists halted the Greek advance but failed at that point to drive the Greeks back. However, Kemal had protected his eastern and southern borders and was free to concentrate on moving north and west against the Greeks. A stalemate developed and during that time the Greek government collapsed and was replaced by a monarchy. Kemal utilized this time by successfully reaching agreements with the Bolshevik government in Russia, with the Italians, and with the French. The terms of these agreements all differed but they each secured

Kemal's nationalists from fear of attacks by more powerful potential adversaries. The Greeks, encouraged by Lloyd George's government, organized a large force in August of 1921 to assault Ankara, which was the center of nationalist strength and Kemal's headquarters. After three bloody weeks of fighting, the Greeks were forced to retreat and were never again the superior force in Turkey.

The British had been occupying Constantinople and the Dardanelles with a nominal force since the end of the war but now could see a substantial army developing to the south and west. The nationalist army had the overwhelming support of the Turkish people and represented a huge struggle even for the British. Lloyd George urged war with the nationalists to retain those sites that the Peace Conference had given to Britain to defend. However, his Cabinet did not agree and, more importantly, the British people, exhausted by a terrible war, would not have supported a new war.

Kemal moved quickly while the British pondered what to do. On August 26, 1922, Turkish forces launched a powerful attack on the Greeks all along the Mediterranean coast. The Greeks suffered a devastating defeat and were forced to evacuate from Smyrna under heavy assault.

The Turks did not cover themselves with glory after the victory because much horrible vengeance was meted out to those Greeks remaining. Kemal pressed his advantage by moving north to the outskirts of Constantinople. He prudently halted and awaited the British decision.

Lloyd George's government was defeated in November 1922 because of this issue of potential war and other matters. The British commander in Constantinople refused to fire on the Turks, and that made the question to negotiate even easier to make. By late 1922 Mustafa Kemal was very famous throughout both the eastern and western worlds and was beloved by most Turks. He was on the brink of creating a fully independent Muslim nation in a world dominated by Christian powers. There was even a small movement to name him the new Sultan, but this concept completely contradicted his beliefs and purposes. Still, the six centuries old sultanate was revered by many so Kemal expressed his views in no uncertain terms: "The reason you do not find the Greek king among our prisoners of war is that royal sovereigns are inclined to partake only of their nation's pleasures. In times of catastrophe, they think of nothing but their palaces."

But the matter of the Sultan was complicated because the symbolic religious leader in Islam was the caliph, whose position had been fused with the sultanate several centuries earlier. To abolish the Sultanate it would be necessary to separate the caliphate, which had no governmental authority, from the Sultan. The Turkish Grand National Assembly, of which Kemal was the undisputed leader, debated this question of separation until Kemal again expressed a clear direction: "Now the Turkish nation...seizes its own sovereignty. This is a fait accompli. If the Assembly accepts this naturally, it would be better in my opinion. If not, this truth will be expressed in due course, although probably some heads will be cut off." Debate ended immediately and the proposal to separate the caliphate from the Sultanate passed quickly. These unambiguous and threatening remarks foretold the autocratic form of governance intended by Mustafa Kemal. The Sultan was allowed to be exiled on a British warship in November of 1922.

By 1923, most of the decisions made in Paris in 1919 dealing with the Ottoman Empire were undone, and the new independent Turkish Nation was recognized by all the world powers.

Until his death in 1938, Kemal energetically moved his new nation to be more westernized in virtually every way. These reforms included: adoption of the Gregorian calendar; banning the Ottoman script; adoption of a constitution requiring a western style legal system; encouragement of western style dress for men and women; support for the emancipation of women, including the right to vote and hold office by 1930; and major changes in the quality of education, particularly in science and technology. In November of 1934, the Turkish Grand National Assembly honored Kemal with the surname "Ataturk," to be properly known from that point forward as "Mustafa Kemal Ataturk."

Turkey in more recent years has become a powerful nation and member of NATO (North Atlantic Treaty Organization). It remains the only truly secular government in the Islamic world and may soon become a full member of the European Union.

Chapter 4. The Russian Revolution and Fear of the Spread of Communism

Lenin and the Bolsheviks

*A*s noted above with regard to Ataturk and the Turkish Revolution, it is *rare when* one man can cast so long a shadow over so many millions of people and such a large land area, but such was also the case with Vladimir Lenin and his impact on Russia. The basic contours of the communist system fashioned by Lenin remained intact for about 70 years. Not only was he indispensable in bringing Bolshevism to power, but he inspired and guided the organization of the communist movement, and he, more than anyone else, shaped the soviet system of rule during the first six years of its existence. Soviet means "councils of workers." Soviet leaders after Lenin's death in 1924 followed in detail the lines set down by the architect of the revolution. For over six decades soviet leaders considered Lenin's teachings to be sacrosanct and persistently invoked his name to justify their policies.

By January 1917, Russia was effectively out of the war and labor strikes, poverty and famine were rampant all over the country. On March 10th, an estimated 200,000 people marched peacefully in St. Petersburg demanding bread and governmental reforms. The Tsar, who understood only autocratic rule, ordered his troops to fire on the demonstrators. Both officers and soldiers refused to do so, and the Tsar was forced to abdicate on March 15th. The leaders who remained formed a Provisional Government, but from the moment of its creation rival centers of authority challenged the government for control. The two principal groups were the Mensheviks and the Bolsheviks who had much in common but also important points of difference.

The Mensheviks consisted of a wide range of political parties, former officers of the imperial army, and nationalists who wished to secure independence. The Mensheviks believed the ultimate socialist revolution would be led by the bourgeois elements of society and not the proletariat workers. These groups were informally referred to as the "Whites."

The Bolsheviks were led by Lenin and an important revolutionary military leader Leon Trotsky. Their group consisted mostly of workers, former soldiers and sailors, and peasants from the countryside. Like the Mensheviks, the Bolsheviks, commonly called the "Reds," were socialists, but unlike the Whites they were also devoted communists and followers of Marxist philosophy. In July of 1917, a spontaneous outpouring of people, estimated to be 500,000, demanded an end to the war and removal of the Provisional Government. Lenin had been in exile in Switzerland and had returned in secret on April 9, 1917, but was unprepared at that point to take advantage of the situation. He realized he had missed an opportunity and determined that that would not happen again. Later in the year, the Reds were much better organized with units of the Red Guard numbering over 25,000. On October 24th, the revolution was launched in St. Petersburg, and with virtually no resistance the Bolsheviks controlled the centers of power in the city. Lenin quickly announced a series of policies that he knew would be instantly popular. The most important was the land program transferring certain property rights from the nobility to the peasants. This was administered by a collection of Soviet Land Commissions. Land ownership remained with the state but peasants were given exclusive rights to farm the land, at least for the present.

However, Lenin did have to contend with growing political and military opposition to his regime in the beginning. From 1918 to late 1920 a brutal civil war raged in the country. By the spring of 1921, the Reds had defeated the Whites and had reestablished a semblance of order in most of what had been the Russian Empire. But there were important losses; Finland, Estonia, Latvia, Lithuania, and Poland all became independent states.

After the military victory, Lenin made it clear that he wanted autocratic powers, and he began that effort by suppressing newspapers and other forms of dissent. He also created a security police force with broad powers of arrest and even secret murders of opponents. The writing was clearly on the wall as to what was coming for the next four decades.

Economic reform was very high on the list of important governmental reforms both because of the philosophical tenets of communism but, more urgently, because of the disastrous state of the economy. In October of 1921, Lenin wisely backpedaled some on communist principles and explained his thinking in a statement on the first New Economic Policy (NEP): "Let us industrialize everything. Capitalists will be amongst us, foreign capitalists, concessionaires, and lease holders: they will wrest from us hundreds per cent of profit, they will flourish around us. Let them flourish; we will learn from them how to carry on industry, and then we shall be able to construct our Communist Republic." This level of pragmatism was necessary but, unfortunately for the Russian economy, was not followed very long because Lenin died early in 1924.

For four years the leaders of the Soviet Union (officially, the Union of Soviet Socialist Republics), violently struggled for power. This centered on a struggle between Trotsky and Joseph Stalin. It was not only a power struggle but an ideological one as well. Trotsky was true to Marx's principles of expanded revolution to bring communism to all industrialized countries. Stalin was more interested in consolidating control over Russia. Trotsky fully believed in Lenin's economic ideas of a minor level of capitalism within the NEP. Stalin viewed this as weakness. Stalin proved to be the more devious and secret manipulator of power centers, and by 1929 he had forced Trotsky and his supporters to leave Russia. Stalin arranged to have Trotsky murdered in Mexico on August 20, 1940. The Soviet Union under Stalin became totalitarian and the government sought to secure total control over national institutions and over people's affairs, private as well as public. No significant initiatives or policies were undertaken without the expressed approval of Stalin, the dictator.

Stalin – The Supreme Leader and the Great Purges

Stalin was born into a poor family in the border republic of Georgia and, unlike other early Bolshevik leaders, had not spent a long period in exile in other parts of Europe. He had much less education, was not intellectually inclined, and had no real internationalist leanings. However, he was very well organized, hard working, and brutal. He was even criticized by Lenin for excessive brutality, but Lenin did not dismiss him. Stalin became the Communist Party general secretary, a post that party intellectuals disdained and thought of as merely administrative. But his mastery of the position gave him exceptional power within the party to approve and disapprove of membership for lower level leaders.

The Soviet system had at least three interrelated centers of power that kept it functioning for about six decades: the Communist Party, the Secret Police and a system of incentives. Substantial rewards were given to loyal and energetic party members, especially those who rose to the upper reaches of the organization. They would receive faster promotions, more spacious apartments, attractive summer homes, admission for their children into the best schools, and other benefits.

Communist economic theory, as preached by Lenin and practiced by Stalin, involved a concept of a totally controlled economy with no opportunities for personal profits based on individual initiative. A good example of this is the collective farm. The government initiated a policy of collectivization of the agricultural sector meant to eliminate individual farms and merge them into large collective farms. The collectives were expected to be much more efficient than small private farms, and Soviet leaders planned to move the excess manpower to the cities. Huge numbers of Russian peasants resisted the authorities with every weapon at their disposal and class warfare spread across much of the countryside. During a two-year span from 1930 to 1931 approximately 400,000 households (roughly two million people) were forcibly deported from the countryside. The disruptions in the villages greatly reduced agricultural output and caused widespread famines.

The government did make some concessions to the peasants. They allowed some of them to have small private plots of land and to work both the collective farm and their own plots. Ironically, this two-fold arrangement demonstrated the effectiveness of economic incentives because the yields from the private land typically amounted to more than six times the yields of the collectives.

The management of state-owned industrial production moved much faster and more successfully than the agricultural collectivization. By the early 1930s, heavy industries such as iron, steel, tool making, electricity generating stations, and manufacturing facilities were expanding rapidly. Untrained workers from the countryside were becoming trained, or in some cases shipped out to distant work camps where the conditions were miserable. In spite of that, in a surprisingly short time the country could boast of having entirely new industries that produced tractors, automobiles, agricultural machinery, and airplanes.

Another aspect of Marxist philosophy that Stalin followed aggressively was Marx's attitude about religion. Marx famously said religion was the "opium of the people." Both Lenin and Stalin firmly agreed, and all religious practices were banned. This was not as difficult as we in the west might imagine because for centuries in Russia the Orthodox religious leaders had supported the Tsar and the nobility. Between 1926 and 1937 the number of Orthodox priests in the Soviet Union decreased by half and the same was true, or worse, for Jewish rabbis, Catholic priests, Protestant ministers, and Muslim Imans. The clergy were not just removed but sometimes were arrested and even murdered. Churches were despoiled and turned into museums; schools and the press were exploited and forced to vilify religion.

The Stalinist purges of 1936 to 1938 undoubtedly marked the most infamous period in Soviet history. Hundreds of thousands of people were arrested for nothing more than suspicion of anti-revolutionary activity or writings. Mere association with those suspected was sufficient for long-term imprisonment. No opportunity to defend oneself was offered, and many never returned from labor camps in Siberia. Historians have questioned why Stalin engaged in such horrific slaughter of his own people, especially at this time when he was in such firm control. No definitive answer is available. It may well be that Stalin had become paranoid believing that everyone was a potential enemy and only by eliminating many could he be certain of including the few true threats. Moreover, the whole population would be so terrorized that no independent thought or action would again take place. A few statistics will reveal the scope of Stalin's war against his own military leaders. About half of the entire officer corps of the army, 35,000 men, were arrested; including 113 out of 115 army commanders, 220 out of 406 brigade commanders, and all eleven vice commissars of war. Some were executed immediately, and others were imprisoned for long periods in corrective labor camps, called "gulags." By Stalin's death in March of 1953, the best estimates of the number of Russians eliminated in the Soviet Union during his term in power amounted to ten to twelve million people.

Having largely decimated his army leadership by 1938, Stalin now faced the most powerful military in Europe – Germany to the west. With war becoming a virtual certainty in the next year, he also correctly assumed that Britain and France would let the Soviets carry the major burden of defending against Germany. The Soviet Union needed time to prepare. Hitler also knew by mid-1939 that he would invade Poland, an action that likely would trigger the guarantees of protection Britain and France had agreed to provide to Poland through the Treaty of Versailles. While British and French defense of Poland was not a certainty, Hitler needed a nonaggression pact with the Soviets as much as Stalin needed one.

To the shock of the western world, on August 23, 1939, Hitler and Stalin announced an agreement that each would remain neutral in the event that the other was attacked. Hitler achieved his primary objective by ensuring a peaceful eastern border when war on the western front began.

Stalin bought the time he needed to build up the military. It strains credulity to think that either of these unscrupulous dictators trusted the other, but the pact at least solved short-term issues for both.

Every bit as important as the publicly disclosed aspects of the agreement, were the secret provisions in which the two countries agreed to divide Poland after the German invasion. Germany would regain Danzig and the western territories of Poland, while the Soviet Union would occupy the Baltic States and most of eastern Poland. The independent state of Poland would simply cease to exist.

Britain and France observed the Hitler-Stalin agreement with mixed feelings. Certainly the neutralization of the Soviets on Germany's eastern front was a very serious military problem for those fighting in the west. Furthermore, it was clear to everyone that the Russians could not put up a serious fight for at least two years in any event. On the other hand, the European capitalist countries were nearly as fearful of the rapid spread of communism from the Soviet Union. Stalin's brutal purges of the last few years were reasonably well known (perhaps not to their full extent) throughout Europe as well. Germany constituted the strongest bulwark against that threat. In 1939 there were still a few who believed that Hitler could be satisfied or, at least, mollified.

Chapter 5. The Rise of Fascism – Italy, Germany and Spain

Mussolini – Drive to Absolutism

The term fascism is frequently used to describe a number of right-wing dictatorships, but the word derives from *Fasci di combattimento* meaning "Bands of Combat." It was used as the name of an Italian political party started in 1919 and composed largely of war veterans and workers. It was also a political philosophy that encompassed anti-democracy, anti-Marxism, and often anti-Semitism. The fascist governments were usually single party dictatorships characterized by terrorism and police surveillance. These movements also championed the cult of a great leader.

Benito Mussolini (1883-1945) was an opportunist of the first order. He could change his ideas and principles to suit every new occasion. Action for him was always more important than thought or rational justification. In his early career, Mussolini was a socialist, and he formed a newspaper with a strong leftist leaning. It was called *Il Popolo d'Italia (The People of Italy)*, but later he discovered that many upper and middle class Italians feared the loss of their property and had no sympathy for socialism or the workers that it protected. They wanted order. As a result, Mussolini changed his philosophy, adopted fascism, and took direct action in the face of government inaction.

By 1920 the Italian Fascists were determined to crush the socialists. They formed local squads of terrorists who disrupted Socialist Party meetings, and beat up their leaders and supporters. Conservative landowners and businessmen were grateful. Fascism, despite being still highly local in its base and organization, began to exhibit the first signs of a national appeal and purpose. Two years later, the Fascists expanded their intimidation to local government officials in northern cities, especially Milan. By October, Mussolini could count hundreds of thousands of supporters, and he led them on a peaceful march on Rome. King Victor Emmanuel III refused to authorize the army to stop the marchers and within weeks asked Mussolini to become Prime Minister. On November 23, 1922, the King and Parliament granted Mussolini dictatorial authority for one year to bring order to local and regional government.

Always a concern in Italian politics was the influence of the Vatican. The Church, while holding no real power, did have significant influence over various segments of Italian society. The Fascist movement benefited by the death in January 1922 of Pope Benedict XV who had opposed all oppressive regimes, especially the Fascists and the Bolsheviks. He was succeeded by the Archbishop of Milan who took the name Pius XI. Mussolini and his northern associates immediately did their best to ingratiate themselves with the new Pope. This paid dividends later in 1929 when the Lateran Treaty between Mussolini's government and the Vatican was signed. It recognized the Vatican as a sovereign state and guaranteed non-interference by the Church in Italian governmental matters. It brought Mussolini badly needed respect and silence about his authoritarian regime. The Treaty was later used as a model in other countries, including Germany.

By 1926, all political parties other than the Fascists were dissolved and Mussolini transformed Italy into a dictatorial state. Many respectable Italians tolerated and even admired Mussolini because they believed he had saved them from Bolshevism. Another area of importance was the suppression of the press. Established independent Roman newspapers were falsely accused of encouraging two assassination attempts on Mussolini. There has always been some doubt about the second; it may well have been staged. These newspapers were closed down and their property was destroyed. Then, very cleverly, the Fascists closed all newspapers but offered to allow them to reopen with generous government loans, if they would toe the line. They all did, and the government had a loyal press.

No sooner had Mussolini achieved unquestioned autocratic powers, neutralized the Vatican, and silenced the press than he faced an international problem that he could not resolve. The economic depression of the 1930s affected all industrialized countries, including Italy. Virtually all European countries were deeply in debt with most loans being held by United States lenders. When the American stock exchange declined precipitously at the end of 1929, European loans were called in and many defaulted, thus exacerbating the problem on both sides of the Atlantic. However, the Italian government was better prepared than most because Mussolini had created a planned economy that linked private ownership of capital to government arbitration of labor disputes. Major industries were organized into syndicates and the government had a strong influence over the kind and quantity of production. This corporate state allowed the government to direct much of the nation's economic life without a formal change of ownership. Later, in 1935, Mussolini attacked and occupied Ethiopia, further justifying placing the country on a wartime economy with even tighter governmental controls.

Hitler – Rise to Power and Pre-War Developments

In Germany in the early 1920s, inflation was destroying society and the standard of living to which most Germans had grown accustomed. One American dollar was worth approximately 800 million German marks. In other words, German currency was worthless. Late in 1923 Adolf Hitler (1889-1945) made his first major appearance on the German political scene. Hitler absorbed much of the rabid German nationalism, racism, and extreme anti-Semitism that flourished in Vienna, Austria, where he lived at that time. His party became known as The National Socialist German Workers Party, simply known as the Nazis. The party platform called for repudiation of the Versailles Treaty, the unification of Austria and Germany, and the exclusion of Jews from German citizenship. The word "socialist" in the party's name was a sham. Because of the economic depression, the extreme political parties, especially the Nazis, gained considerable support among war veterans and unemployed workers who experienced economic and social displacement.

As Hitler established his dominance in the Nazi Party, he clearly had the model of Mussolini in mind and spoke of the Italian dictator's accomplishments in glowing terms. On November 9, 1923, Hitler and a band of followers attempted a *putsch* (sudden political revolt) from a beer hall in Munich. When the local authorities crushed the attempted uprising, Hitler and others were arrested and tried for treason. Although Hitler used the trial to make himself into a national figure, he was convicted and sentenced to five years in prison. He was paroled after serving only a few months. During his time in prison, Hitler wrote *Mein Kampf (My Struggle)* where he outlined key political views including fierce anti-Semitism, opposition to Bolshevism, and a conviction that Germany must expand eastward into Poland and Ukraine. Thus, those Germans who professed later to be unaware of Hitler's intentions and ultimate direction were clearly either extremely uninformed or attempting to justify their complaisance.

Hitler's rise to power was far more complicated and took much longer than Mussolini's but was no less absolute in achieving dictatorial powers. The German government of the 1920s consisted of a parliament, called the Reichstag, which was fairly weak, a president, Field Marshall Paul von Hindenburg, (a General in World War I), and a chancellor appointed by the president who, like a prime minister, held most of the powers. As previously noted, the decade of the 1920s was extremely difficult economically for Germany, and the government, known as the Weimar Republic, had little success in improving the economy until about 1926. But again in 1932, German unemployment had risen to over six million, mostly among youths, with no improvement in sight. The Nazis held mass rallies and gained powerful supporters in business, the military, and publishing circles.

President von Hindenburg, at the age of 83, announced in 1932 that he would run again for president. Hitler's goal was not the presidency but the chancellorship, where the real power resided. He knew though that Hindenburg would not appoint him chancellor and, in fact, had negative personal views toward Hitler. He often referred to him as the "house painter." Hitler was persuaded by his followers to oppose Hindenburg and run for president. Although he lost the election, he received 30% of the vote in the first balloting and 37% in the runoff election. The Nazi Party won 230 seats in the Reichstag, which amounted to the largest voting block in the legislature. Hitler demanded to be appointed chancellor. Hindenburg refused and appointed Franz von Papen, a weak and extremely conservative associate of the President. Hitler was privately offered the vice-chancellorship but he refused. Hitler informed the President's representatives that he had dedicated himself to wiping out the Marxist parties and that this could not be done unless he took over the government and ran things his own way. He added that one could not shy away from bloodshed and asked, mockingly, if the King of Italy had offered Mussolini the vice-chancellorship after the march on Rome. There were several conversations directly between Hindenburg and Hitler, but neither would budge from his position. Hindenburg was finding it impossible to form a government without the participation of the Nazis. He was also being besieged by supporters among the finance, industrial, and military establishments to appoint Hitler as chancellor. They saw in Hitler order, economic development, and strong resistance to communism. The final straw for Hindenburg was when Hitler demanded new elections to determine who would be chancellor. He very reluctantly appointed Hitler as chancellor on January 30, 1933.

Once in office, Hitler moved rapidly to consolidate his control. This process involved three steps: the capture of full legal authority, the crushing of alternative political groups, and the purging of rivals within the Nazi party itself. By March of 1933, the Reichstag passed an Enabling Act that permitted Hitler to rule by decree. A few months later, in June and July, all other German political parties were outlawed, and the Nazis were now the only legal party in Germany and Hitler was their unchallenged leader.

Although publicly unchallenged, Hitler was still concerned about secret cabals against his leadership, particularly in the SA, a paramilitary organization within the Nazi party. The SA, also known as the *brownshirts*, was headed by Ernst Roehm, a former military officer who had supported Hitler from the beginning. Roehm wanted to have control, or at least parity, with the formal German military who, of course, strongly resisted any such concepts. Hindenburg was still a revered figure among the military, and Hitler did not want further confrontations with the President. Hitler knew that any long-term control of the country would require the full support of the German army. It has never been clear that Roehm led a conspiracy against Hitler, but some high elements of the SA were certainly resisting party direction. After much internal consternation, Hitler agreed with his principal advisors to move against the SA leadership, and in one weekend of June 30 – July 2, 1934 rounded up more than 200 SA leaders and others suspected of collaboration, including Roehm. Approximately 100 were executed, along with Roehm, who professed his loyalty to Hitler to the end. One month later, President Hindenburg died of natural causes, and Hitler had the Reichstag combine the offices of president and chancellor. He now held dictatorial power over all of Germany including the Wehrmacht, the combined military forces. Later, all members of the military were required to make pledges of loyalty, not just to the country but to Adolf Hitler personally.

By the mid-1930s, the German economy had recovered dramatically. The reasons were twofold: its industrial base had not been damaged during the first war, and Hitler's government was embarked on a huge military buildup, increasingly in violation of the Versailles Treaty. This should not have been a surprise to anyone since Hitler had long ago expressed his intention not to honor the Treaty, especially the military rebuilding restrictions. German militarization moved faster and faster as Hitler tested the will of the French and British to restrain it. Both governments were found to be unwilling to take any action. One exception to this was Winston Churchill who warned often that Hitler could not be trusted

Also during this time, the anti-Semitism of the Nazis and other Germans became increasingly virulent. In 1933 Jews were prohibited from all civil service, and in 1935 they were robbed of their citizenship. Jewish owned businesses were being harassed and in some cases confiscated. This was happening in plain sight but with no significant complaint from either the German people or the various Christian churches. On November 9-10 of 1938, Hitler and the Nazis showed the true colors of their racial prejudice when Jewish stores and synagogues were burned and otherwise destroyed in what is known as *"Kristallnacht"* (Crystal Night).

On the international scene, Hitler followed a process he used in the political and economic arenas by taking small steps initially but never backing down or wavering from his stated goals. One of these involved the Rhineland, which was part of Germany on the border with France but west of the Rhine River. The Versailles Treaty allowed Germany to retain this land but required that it be a demilitarized zone. Hitler simply sent troops to occupy the Rhineland in 1936 and, although the French complained, they did nothing about it. Next Hitler demanded the return of the Sudetenland, an area previously part of Germany but awarded to Czechoslovakia under the terms of the Treaty. The Czechs objected and requested assistance from France and Britain. A conference in Munich was held in September of 1938. It was attended by Neville Chamberlain of Britain, Edouard Daladier of France, Italian representatives, and Hitler, but not the Czechs. The British and French gave in completely to Hitler and only obtained his promise that he had no further territorial claims. Chamberlain returned to England and proclaimed they had achieved "peace in our time." The term *appeasement* has ever since been associated with this agreement.

But the following year, 1939, demonstrated even more dramatic Nazi demands. Hitler capitalized further on the German anger about decisions made by the Allied leaders in Paris in 1919, specifically the loss of the German city, Danzig, in the east Prussian area. The Treaty changed the city into a free port city with unrestricted access from the Baltic to the reestablished independent Poland. The vast majority of German citizens supported the reinstatement of Danzig as an integral part of Germany. It wasn't long after the agreement at Munich in September 1938 that Hitler began demanding that Danzig and the whole transportation corridor south to Poland be placed under exclusive German control. The Poles vigorously opposed any change and demanded support from Britain and France. However, German military forces in 1939 had been virtually restored to their levels before World War I, so Hitler was determined, at some point soon, to occupy Danzig and invade Poland.

But there were many uncertainties. Perhaps first and foremost was the reaction of Stalin and the Soviet Union to German troops at or near the Russians' western border. The Soviets were short of military leadership and otherwise unprepared for a major war. Stalin needed time. But Hitler had serious concerns as well. Ever since the days of Bismarck in the previous century, German leaders had been worried about a two front war. Of course, this is exactly what happened in World War I. Consequently, Hitler promoted a very quick, non-aggression pact with Stalin that was signed on August 23, 1939. The basic terms were previously covered, but from Hitler's viewpoint, it guaranteed no military resistance from the Soviets when he invaded Poland.

Hitler was still convinced, because of the opinions of his foreign policy advisors, that Britain and France would not wage a large European war to save Poland. So with his east protected and an unjustified optimism about the western powers, Germany invaded Poland on September 1, 1939. Two days later Britain and France declared war and World War II had begun.

Spanish Fascism and Civil War

If one were to draw sides as a prelude to the next great war, one could hardly do better than to consider the Spanish Civil War which broke out in 1936. As the war in Spain advanced in the next two years, the Allied powers, Russia and

France, sided with the elected, socialist/communist government, while Germany and Italy sided with the revolutionary fascists under General Francisco Franco. But Spain was different from all the other western European powers because it had remained neutral during World War I and, therefore, was in much better condition economically. It profited from extensive international markets, which encouraged its business leaders to push for more capitalist reforms, improve conditions of the working class, and reduce the dominance of the agrarian sector.

The first Republic had been declared in 1931 after King George was forced into exile because of his resistance to any change seen by many to be necessary to modernize the country. The new government consisted of an odd combination of liberal republicans, socialists, intellectuals, and nationalists who wanted greater local autonomy. One thing that united these disparate groups was aggressive anticlerical legislation. The Catholic Church in Spain had for centuries associated itself with reactionary forces of the old regime, especially the monarchy, and opposed all liberalism and modernization. The governments that followed implemented many reforms both democratic and economic, but could not unify the plethora of parties that were active. When national elections were held in February 1936, a new group called the Spanish Popular Front won most positions in the government. This party was made up of leftists, communists, and anarchists. This was too much for the conservative military leaders who lacked only a strong leader and admired the models of totalitarian fascism in Italy and Germany. General Franco filled that void quickly and formed an army in Spanish Morocco in the south, across from Gibraltar. In July his army, known generally as the "Fascists," began to move north through the center of Spain with a goal to take Madrid rapidly. That did not happen.

Franco was supported by Hitler and Mussolini's fascist governments with weapons, artillery, and even tanks and airplanes. In some cases, the planes were piloted by German pilots. The Popular Front government was initially supported by the Soviet Union and later by France but never to the extent supplied by the Axis powers. The Civil War took on a romantic aura because of the stark ideological contrasts between liberal and conservative economic and political models. Socialism and communism were far more popular in the mid 1930s than today, and many western ideologues, like Ernest Hemingway, came to Spain to volunteer to help the elected Popular Front government.

France had the most to lose from a Franco victory because it would place hostile fascist powers to its south as well as its east. However, ironically, France did very little practically to assist the leftist government. Even as late as the second half of the 1930s, there was still nearly as much fear of the spread of communism from Russia as there was fear of Nazi Germany. These dual fears had the effect of paralyzing government decision making and giving rise to unwarranted optimism and appeasement. The British were also not of one mind regarding Franco; did he represent a threat or a protection of British interests? British diplomatic correspondence in July of 1936 stated one view: "Everyone anxiously awaits result of General Franco's *coup d'etat*. Should he fail, I believe dangerous disorders are bound to occur in (Spain)." (Consul Harold Patteson)

In an effort to localize the conflict in Spain, the British, French, and US governments urged all interested countries to informally join a Non-Intervention agreement, pledging not to arm or otherwise assist either side in the Civil War. Germany and Italy immediately agreed and then continued their support of Franco. The Soviets, at least, did not play the sham, ignoring the non-intervention effort and continuing their support of the Popular Front government. Stalin was having some success in organizing the International Brigades, who were foreign fighters committed to leftist causes in several countries and who enthusiastically came to Spain to fight the fascists. This international involvement was consistent with Marxist principles of the spread of communism around the developed world and, of course, reinforced the opinions of those whose greatest fear was the communist movement.

Most observers of the war in late 1936 fully expected Franco to take control of Madrid by the end of the year. However, after fierce fighting and much destruction in the City, the Popular Front and their leftist supporters held out, and Franco ended the assault of the city on November 22nd. Franco then split his army moving one group northeast to reach the Mediterranean about 100 miles south of Barcelona, and the other group advanced north to reach the Basque area on the French border. By now it was clear that the Fascists could not be defeated, and even a long holdout by the Popular Front would require far greater support from outside sources.

However, in early 1938, the attention of all of Europe was focused on the Nazi threat, and very few leaders concerned themselves with Spain. The respected American historian, Philip Minehan, has described the atmosphere in Europe at this time: "The drive behind the firm Nazi and Italian Fascist commitment to a Spanish rebel victory was, first of all, part of the pan-European momentum of fascism on the offensive, spurred on by the appeasement of it by the liberal democracies led by Great Britain. The recklessly experimental and aggressively expansionistic characters of the Third Reich and Fascist Italy required dramatic political-military successes both for their domestic and international prestige and fearsomeness."

Perhaps capitalizing on this reduced attention, Franco aggressively and brutally attacked city after city until in January 1939 Barcelona fell and Franco consolidated his armies for a second attack on Madrid. The capital City was taken with no resistance on March 27th. Four days later Franco announced, "Today, with the Red Army captive and disarmed...the war is over." Final numbers of dead, wounded, and displaced in this three-year civil war have never really been available, but informed estimates suggest several hundred thousand. When the Second World War began, Spain quickly announced its neutrality but secretly helped Germany with intelligence and other important assistance.

More recently, since the 1960s, there have been significant liberalizations and economic development and a return to a constitutional monarchy. During Franco's rule these changes decisively reduced his dictatorial powers and strengthened his opposition. Moreover, the Catholic Church functioned more freely after Vatican II and saw an increase in younger clergy. Later, Spain entered the European Union and in 2002 adopted the euro as its currency. (More about this in a later chapter.)

Chapter 6. World War II – European Theater

Early Actions of the Nazis

After the western powers were intimidated by Hitler at Munich in September of 1938, he became increasingly convinced that they were mostly words and not action. His primary goal in 1939 was the absorption back into Germany of the City of Danzig and the elimination of the Polish corridor. Once Hitler accomplished his non-aggression pact with Stalin, he felt no restraint in moving against Poland. Essentially, this agreement doomed Poland because the Soviets, in effect, agreed not to intervene if Germany attacked Poland. On September 1, 1939, the Nazis did just that. In a matter of a few weeks, the Germans had taken control of most of Poland and the City of Danzig. They then began to divide up certain territories for the Soviets, including Estonia, Lithuania, and Latvia on the Baltic, and parts of Poland bordering the Soviet Union. On September 3, 1939, Britain and France surprised Hitler by declaring war on Germany and World War II began.

The early months of the war in the west saw complete German victories in Denmark, Netherlands, and a little later, Belgium. Their success in Norway, however, was not so fast or easy. Norway was a strategically important country for Germany because it offered protection to the "Homeland" from the north and provided excellent deep-water ports on the North Sea for German warships to move out into the Atlantic. An important disadvantage was that it was close (about 400 miles) from the main British naval base at Scapa Flow, Scotland. From the earliest days of the war the superior British Navy constantly patrolled and dominated the North Sea.

The British, in their own interest, were quick to assist the Norwegians, even sending troops to invade the northwestern part of the country. But the Germans had succeeded in occupying the more populous and important south, including Oslo. Numerous skirmishes occurred making it clear to most observers that British troops were not properly led, trained, or equipped. There were, however, several fierce naval battles between German and British destroyers off the Norwegian coast. Two capital ships, the German cruiser *Blucher* and the British carrier *Glorious*, were both sunk with the loss of nearly 1,000 on each side. The

British eventually withdrew and the Nazis occupied Norway to nearly the end of the war. During the fighting the Germans lost about 5,300 to the British losses of 4,500.

Although Finland was never a part of the German–Soviet pact, Stalin saw this as an opportune time to move against the lightly populated land to the north. Helsinki was only a short distance across the Baltic from Leningrad and would have been an excellent point from which to attack, if occupied by a hostile government. Finland also had large sources of nickel so necessary in arms manufacture. In October of 1939, Stalin demanded complete control of all important areas of Finland, but the Finns immediately rejected the demands. Stalin believed no tiny population of 3.6 million could possibly resist the huge Soviet Union. But the Finns were a very proud people and relished their independence. A local joke at the time expressed the spirit of the people: "They (Russian troops) are so many and our country is so small, where shall we find room to bury them all."

Finland is mountainous with narrow, often snow-covered primitive passageways. Although the Soviets had tanks and motorized vehicles, they were constantly attacked from high positions, often with light, easily transported weapons such as machine guns and gasoline bombs. The Soviets made advances into Finland but always at great cost in personnel and equipment. One assault in January 1940 received attention and much praise in the west. The Russians attacked with 4,000 troops against only 32 well-positioned Finns. The Russians prevailed but lost 400 men to 28 Finns. The Finnish army occasionally counterattacked, but their victories were short-lived. The war ground on in 1940 without significant change until the Soviets realized later in the year that a far greater menace was building on their western border. Stalin's co-conspirator in aggression was moving millions of soldiers and equipment east to the Russian border.

The battle for France began in earnest in the spring of 1940. Once his northern border was protected with the defeat of Norway, Hitler advanced his *Wehrmacht* (defense force) quickly on a long front into France. The French relied on the so called "Maginot Line" which was a defense line of heavy fortifications reminiscent of World War I trenches, but far more sophisticated. The French military leadership was also burdened with concepts and plans long outdated and which had been none too successful in the last war.

The mechanized German army moved very quickly, penetrating the defenses and capturing hundreds of thousands of French troops from behind. For the most part, it was not a case, as some historians have alleged, of French soldiers' reluctance to fight but a total failure of modern military competence by the French generals. The fastest German movement was in the north through Belgium and then a straight line to Paris. By June of 1940 the German occupation of all of northern France, including Paris, was inevitable, and the government decided to surrender rather than to see its beloved city destroyed. The Germans allowed a collaborator government to be established in the south of France with a capital at Vichy. This area was known as Vichy France and was completely subordinate to Hitler.

Prior to total German occupation, the British arranged a courageous removal of their soldiers and many thousands of French soldiers from the Belgian port of Dunkirk. This was accomplished under heavy air attack from the German air force and with the brave volunteer assistance of many small boat owners from Dover across the Channel. It is estimated that in three days of crossings, about 350,000 soldiers were saved to fight another day.

During the winter of 1940 and spring of 1941 the Germans launched air attacks almost daily on Great Britain, and especially London. However, the British resisted at great cost and ultimately stopped Hitler in what is known as the *Battle of Britain*. The Royal Air Force (RAF) defended the home island courageously and destroyed nearly twice as many planes of the Luftwaffe as the RAF lost. The British were greatly aided by the world's first integrated radar system that provided early warning of location, size, and probable targets of the attacking German bombers. This top-secret, scientific advance was not discovered by the Germans until much later in the war. After nearly a year of German bombing attacks, Hitler finally became convinced that he could not subdue Britain through air attacks alone.

Continental Europe was under almost total domination of Germany and Italy until the summer of 1941 when Hitler, flush with victory, breached his agreement with Stalin and invaded the Soviet Union. Many observers have questioned why Hitler chose to attack the Soviets at this time since he was still fighting Britain in the west and Stalin presented no immediate threat to Germany. In retrospect, the decision was a bad one, but after virtually no resistance anywhere in Europe, Hitler believed his Wehrmacht, and more importantly he himself, were invincible. In addition, he observed the great difficulties Stalin had in subduing tiny Finland and concluded that the Soviet Union was a paper tiger. He also knew that Stalin was on a crash course to rebuild his military forces and that waiting probably meant a tougher fight for the Nazis. In any event, *Operation Barbarossa* was launched on June 22, 1941. As Hitler expected, the attack completely surprised Stalin and the German army advanced quickly and deeply into Russia. They reached Leningrad (current St. Petersburg) and the outskirts of Moscow in November. The Germans were able to capture huge numbers of Russian troops, roughly 2.5 million, because of advance planning by the Germans and virtually no planning by the Soviets.

However, the tide turned at the end of the year when the Russian winter, which had so devastated Napoleon in the 19th century and stalled the German army in the prior war, set in. The Nazis were woefully unprepared because they expected to occupy Moscow before winter and, at least psychologically, to end resistance on their eastern front. Hitler delayed a final seizure of the capital city and moved many divisions to the south to capture important oil facilities. With a reprieve of a few months, Stalin reinforced defenses and began to attack German supply lines that were stretched to breaking. The light, fast German mechanized army became mired in mud and snow and was an easy target. The Germans retreated to defensive positions and resolved to renew the attack in the spring.

But another important development occurred at the end of 1941 that changed the whole complexion of the war. The United States declared war on Japan after that nation's attack at Pearl Harbor in the Hawaiian Islands. Within a few days, Germany and the US had exchanged declarations of war, and now Britain was no longer alone in the western front but had an exceptionally powerful, if unprepared, ally in their struggle with Hitler.

American Entry and Final Defeat of Germany

Churchill and his countrymen were certainly happy to have the US with them, at last, to buttress their cause, now in its third year. However, the British soon realized that they were required to give up some elements of control, both military and political. Fortunately, the political leadership of the two countries, Prime Minister Winston Churchill and President Franklin Roosevelt, had an excellent relationship and had actually met on one occasion in New Found-land before the US entry into the war. Directions were given on both sides for full cooperation in military planning and operation. No joint command on such a large scale in a world war had ever been attempted before, and there was certainly no guarantee that this one would succeed. The top military commanders, US General George Marshall and British General Alan Brooke, had a frosty relationship at first, but both eventually came to respect each other and insist that their subordinates cooperate completely.

One early military planning issue that divided the Allies was that of when and where to launch the combined attack on continental Europe. After much discussion, it was agreed that the US would not be ready for such a massive undertaking until 1943. The great difference of opinion about where to attack was a sustained dividing point between the Allies. US planners wanted the invasion to be at the heart of Germany, landing across the Channel in France and moving quickly to the industrial Ruhr Valley in northwest Germany. British planners, actually led by Churchill himself, believed that the German defenses in France were much too formidable and it was wiser to attack the "soft underbelly" in the south – Sicily and Italy. Both positions had merit, but the final determinant was that by the spring of 1943, the US would not have been prepared either with equipment or personnel to launch the attack that it wanted. However, some action was necessary soon to show the home front and the enemy the determination and fighting spirit of the Allies.

In November of 1942, British and US troops launched attacks from the east and the west on German forces in North Africa. The British held Egypt in the east and in October moved west against the Afrika Korps under General Erwin Rommel. Both British and American forces landed at Vichy French Algeria and Morocco in November. The fighting was slow and difficult, but German supplies were nearly cut off by Allied air dominance. The Afrika Korps was defeated in some of the most famous tank battles in history. The Germans ultimately surrendered in May of 1943. This provided an opportunity for the Allies to attack from the south into Italy. At the same time the Russians were holding the German advance at great loss to themselves as well as to the Germans, particularly during the battle of Stalingrad, where Hitler lost over 800,000 troops by death, illness and capture.

British and American forces invaded Sicily in August 1943 and after some resistance moved on to Italy. The fighting and terrain in Italy were exceptionally challenging, and the Allied advance was slowed to a few miles per day. The German army had basically taken over the defense of Italy from the inept Italians. Indeed, Mussolini was thrown out of power in July, and after hiding out for nearly two years, was unceremoniously executed by his own people in April of 1945. The fighting in Italy continued until nearly the end of the war but had the benefit to the Allies of tying up many German divisions that were not then available at Normandy in 1944.

By 1943 the British and the Americans dominated the air and launched devastating attacks on Germany causing the destruction of many German cities, including Cologne, Dresden, and eventually Berlin. The Allies launched "D-Day" on June 6, 1944 by invading the French coast at Normandy. After less than one additional year, the Allies and the Russians defeated the Nazis, who surrendered in May of 1945.

There were many devastating effects of the European portion of the war, but undoubtedly the most horrific was Hitler's "Final Solution" of the Jewish population in Germany, and all the occupied countries. The systematic mass murder, known as the "Holocaust," massacred more than 6 million Jews and other opponents of Hitler in less than seven years. Anti-Semitism was rampant in many parts of Europe before the war, and Hitler succeeded in his racist dementia by unjustly blaming the Jews for virtually all of the problems of Germany in the 1920s and 1930s.

Britain, American and Soviet Discussions

Even before the war was over, Churchill, Roosevelt and Stalin were holding discussions about post-war matters. They were determined not to repeat the mistakes made in Paris in 1919. Churchill and Roosevelt were mostly concerned with Stalin's control of Eastern Europe. An important conference between the big three was held in early February 1945 at Yalta in the Crimea. There, important decisions were reached, which essentially allowed the Soviet Union to dominate all of Eastern Europe and half of Germany, including Berlin. The Allies were to control the western half of Germany and certain sections of the City of Berlin. It was clear that Stalin would have resisted any agreement requiring the Soviet Union to give up control of the territories it had conquered, to the point of war. The Allies were unwilling to continue a massive war against a now very powerful adversary, the Soviet Union.

Clouding some of the discussions was the attitude of Churchill on the need to preserve the British colonies as they had been prior to the war. This view was not shared by Roosevelt, and needless to say, not by Stalin either. At an earlier conference (Tehran, Nov. 1943), Churchill expressed his opinions in characteristically clear terms when he stated that as far as Britain was concerned it did not desire to acquire any new territory or bases, but intended to hold on to what it had. He said that nothing would be taken from England without a war. He mentioned specifically Singapore and Hong Kong. Of course, things changed significantly after the war with India becoming independent in 1947, Singapore in 1965, and Hong Kong in 1997.

The last of the Big Three conferences took place in July and early August of 1945 in a suburb of Berlin called Potsdam. Roosevelt had died in April and President Harry Truman attended for the United States. Many issues were discussed but few were resolved. The principal issue was how to divide Germany, and especially Berlin, among the four allied powers; the US, USSR, Britain, and France. Germany was roughly divided between east and west, and Berlin, wholly within East Germany, was split into four sectors. It was also at this conference that Truman informed Stalin about the successful test of an atomic bomb. Stalin already knew through his intelligence agents, but gave no indication of this.

After the war many types of inventories were taken, but the one statistical fact that shocked the world and many Europeans especially, was the massive production of war materiel generated in a relatively short time by the United States. The US had produced, starting in 1942, more airplanes, ships, tanks, motorized vehicles, bombs, small arms, ammunition, and other materiel than all other combatant countries on both sides combined. One example is worth mentioning: during the war years the US produced 8,812 major naval vessels, while Britain, Germany, the Soviet Union, Italy, and Japan together produced 3,187. The ability of the Allies to quickly replace damaged materiel, often with superior new equipment, was a huge advantage.

Chapter 7. Soviet Threat and NATO

The Emergence of American Influence in Europe

For over a century and a half, most Americans believed their government should heed the words of George Washington as he left the presidency, "Beware of foreign entanglements." By this he meant to avoid treaties and other commitments that could bring the US into war. That advice was followed for the most part until the end of the Second World War when it changed dramatically. Isolationism was finished as a foreign policy and the US had to become a world leader, whether that was a popular policy or not.

During the winter of 1946-47, the worst in memory, Europe seemed on the verge of collapse. In London, coal shortages left only enough fuel to heat and light homes for a few hours a day. In Berlin, the vanquished were freezing and starving to death. European cities were seas of rubble, 500 million cubic yards of it in Germany alone.

In America small groups of individuals, led by George C. Marshall, the Secretary of State, were organizing a relief effort to assist all of Western Europe. The European Recovery Program, better known as the "Marshall Plan," was an extraordinary act of strategic generosity. It amounted to over $100 billion in today's values or about six times what America now spends on foreign aid. The relief got underway in June of 1947 and, according to former Prime Minster Winston Churchill, the Marshall Plan was: "the most unsordid act in history." Marshall's name was connected with it because of his unequalled reputation as the US military's highest-ranking general in the war, referred to by many as the "organizer of victory." Marshall explained the Plan as: "Our policy is not directed against any country or doctrine, but against hunger, poverty, desperation and chaos." By 1948 there were 150 ships per day carrying food and fuel to Europe, and the result was a constant rise in Europe's per capita GNP during the years 1948-51. The Plan also helped America by staving off communism in Western Europe.

In the West some countries, such as France and Italy, were reestablishing democratic republics and containing communism as minority political parties.

The Soviet Union offered a marked contrast, however. The Eastern European countries within the Soviet sphere were governed autocratically through puppet governments controlled from Moscow. The two sides represented two fundamentally different worldviews: one upheld the principles of free enterprise, personal freedom, and popular participation in government. The other upheld one party rule, public ownership of the means of production, state control over all institutions, and economic and social rigidity.

This bitter conflict between the communist and capitalist worlds was commonly referred to as the "cold war," but it was confined to economic, political and military development rivalries, and not actual war. This contrast was never more evident than in the post war divided Germany. The victors agreed to divide Germany roughly in half between east and west. West Germany was controlled by Britain, France, and the United States, and East Germany was dominated by the Soviets. Berlin, being well within the Soviet sector, was also divided nearly in half between east and west. Stalin initially agreed to allow access from the west to Berlin through East Germany. Because of the harshness of Soviet control, ordinary German citizens began to migrate in large numbers from the east to the west. This was especially true in Berlin. To make movement more difficult and to punish West Berliners for their apparent disloyalty, Stalin breached his agreement in June of 1948 and cut off all access to West Berlin from the Allied sectors. The British and Americans responded by supplying West Berlin with essentials such as food, medicine, and fuel by air. Although difficult, this airlift basically broke the Soviet blockade and Stalin lifted it in May of 1949.

While the west was rebuilding in the late 1940s, the Soviet Union was embarking on an economic policy similar to that of its pre-war pattern. The emphasis was on heavy industry to the neglect of consumer goods. The battle cry was to overtake the west in economic production and to produce as quickly as possible an atom bomb. Under intense pressure from Stalin and by stealing nuclear secrets from the US and Britain, the Soviets were able to successfully explode an atom bomb in August 1949. For the next forty years the world would be dominated by two superpowers with nuclear weapons capable of mutual annihilation.

Immediately after the war, the United States developed a foreign policy known as "containment". Also called the Truman Doctrine, it emphasized resistance to Soviet expansion with the expectation that the Soviet Union would collapse from internal economic pressures and the burdens of its foreign oppression. The United States undertook enormous military expenditures and sent large amounts of money abroad. However, the Soviets maintained their dominance over Eastern Europe and East Germany and ultimately built a wall across Eastern Europe to prohibit citizens of those countries from escaping.

The North Atlantic Treaty Organization (NATO) was created in April of 1949 and consisted of Italy, Denmark, Norway, Portugal, Canada and the United States. Later France, Britain, West Germany, Greece and Turkey joined NATO. Its purpose was to establish a commitment between its members to provide mutual assistance, including military assistance if necessary, in the event any member was attacked. As a charter member, the US offered the strongest element of defense to the other members, and for the first time in the nation's history, it had agreed to a major mutual defense treaty. It is consistent with the Truman Doctrine of containment in that it did not threaten action against the Soviet Union unless the Soviets first moved to expand their territory in Europe. The Soviets attempted to counter NATO by creating in May of 1955 their own mutual defense agreement called the "Warsaw Pact." Besides the USSR the Pact included Albania, Bulgaria, Czechoslovakia, East Germany, Hungary, Poland, and Romania – all nations under the thumb of the Soviets.

One country originally included in the Soviet sphere after the war could not be included in the Warsaw Pact, Yugoslavia. The Yugoslav communist regime was controlled by Josip Broz Tito, a universally respected war leader who had challenged Nazi occupation and commanded great popular support. Large numbers of Yugoslavs of all backgrounds were proud of his resistance and many successes against the occupiers. After the war, Tito moved quickly to consolidate several small countries (Soviet style) into one Yugoslavia and under his total control. Initially Stalin tried to dominate Tito, but Tito refused to follow the outdated and failed economic policies of Stalinization. Specifically, he refused to implement agrarian collectivization as directed by Moscow. There were other important differences and, in 1948, Tito led Yugoslavia out of the Soviet Union. Stalin was faced with a serious challenge for the first time from a satellite country. There were several reasons why Stalin did not wish to send the

Red Army into Yugoslavia: Tito and his government had been established by the Yugoslavs themselves and not by the Soviets; Tito was a committed communist, and total loyalty from the Russian Army to move against him was problematic; Tito presented no threat to the Soviets or any of his neighbors; and military domination of Yugoslavia would be very difficult and costly, as the Germans had discovered.

Post Stalin Soviet Union

When on March 5, 1953, the feared and despised Stalin died, some optimistic leaders in the west expected great changes to occur. They were to be disappointed. Nikita Khrushchev was appointed Party Secretary immediately, but the Politburo, the Soviet governing body, was slow to bestow absolute power on any one person. However, Khrushchev maneuvered himself into the Premiership three years later. It was clear then that he was in complete control when he made a secret speech to the Party Congress denouncing the crimes of Stalin in the strongest terms, calling him an enemy of the people. It is not certain if Khrushchev really intended that the speech be kept secret, but in fact, it was translated and published all over the world in a few days. In the early years of Khrushchev's time in power, the mid 1950s to 1964, he attempted economic reforms with mixed results. He ordered the cultivation of vast areas of virgin land requiring the mass movement of hundreds of thousands of workers from urban areas to the new farms. Besides unsettling large numbers of people at both ends, the agricultural production from the new areas was modest at best. Bureaucratic requirements remained and, as an example, if a peasant wanted to slaughter a cow, he had to get permission from no less than seven officials. On the industrial side, Khrushchev also attempted major changes by moving thousands of managers from central offices in Moscow to the plant sites all over the vast country. This might have been a good management initiative if it had been done with better planning and more gradually, but typical of Khrushchev's impetuousness, it was done all at once. The result was chaos and intensive infighting among the top managers. Industrial production did not increase, and in some areas it declined. To a growing number of political elite, Khrushchev appeared to be a man who flitted from one reform to another, and sometimes back again.

Of course Khrushchev was blamed for these failures, and the inner circle of Soviet leaders were not afraid to privately criticize him, as they never would have Stalin. However, he was given an opportunity in November 1956 to assert Soviet control through military power when a grassroots independence revolt developed in Budapest, Hungary. After several days delay, Soviet troops already in the country used heavy weapons including tanks to ruthlessly put down the rebellion. While criticized abroad, Khrushchev was solidly supported at home, especially by a unified military. NATO complained but did nothing. Offsetting the disgrace of the suppression of Hungary, in the world's eyes, were the successful launch in 1957 of the first satellite, *Sputnik*, to orbit the earth, and in 1960, the first manned satellite piloted by Yuri Gagarin.

Unfortunately for Khrushchev these triumphs were not enough to save his Premiership, especially after the disastrous confrontation with America over missiles in Cuba in 1962. Prior to that, he had been required to seek permission from the Presidium to build a wall between the Soviet and western sectors of Berlin to prevent the exodus of Berliners who were moving out to the west. These humiliations were too much for the Soviet power structure. So in October 1964, Khrushchev was summoned to appear before the Central Committee of the Party and was charged with various offenses. Leonid Brezhnev presided, and it was clear to all, including Khrushchev, that Brezhnev had the support to remove him. Unlike the Stalin days when a former high official would have been immediately killed, or at least sent to a *gulag*, Khrushchev was allowed to resign and go into quiet retirement.

Leonid Brezhnev was the premier of the Soviet Union from 1964 to his death in 1982. Brezhnev's eighteen years in power were noteworthy primarily for almost total lack of economic improvement, but a very aggressive foreign policy, especially toward the eastern bloc countries. In looking back, many Russians refer to this period as the "era of stagnation." Brezhnev was not a man of ideas, and certainly not of reform, but he lavished personal benefits on himself and a few close to him. A story, perhaps true, is illustrative: Brezhnev was showing his mother several large, expensive homes that he had acquired, when he asked her what she thought of them. She replied they were very nice -- but what would he do if the communists came back in power?

Although Brezhnev was willing to accept a *détente*, a lessening of tension, with the US, he did not hesitate to enforce Moscow's will throughout the Soviet bloc. In 1968 communist reformers took over the Czechoslovak government. Because they were communists, Brezhnev vacillated for a few months but then came down hard on the rebels. He proclaimed the Brezhnev Doctrine, which basically said the Soviet Union had the right to intervene militarily in any Soviet state that was threatening the welfare of the whole union. Obviously, this made the Cold War even more frigid.

Brezhnev's end came in death, but his power and internal prestige declined precipitously after he launched a costly war in Afghanistan that most Soviet citizens did not understand or support. The army had to endure a humiliating retreat. Because of the war and decades of centralized economic policies, the economy of the Soviet Union was near collapse. During the next few years, until 1985, the country had minimal direction, but then a truly transformational leader was appointed – Mikhail Gorbachev.

Soviet and Allied Espionage

International spying certainly did not begin during the cold war. Both British and Soviet spy networks were very active and quite sophisticated in the 1930s. This time especially provided a fertile environment for the recruitment of those in Britain, mainly intellectuals, who believed the capitalist economic system was not working and would soon be replaced. Of course, this was the time of the worst worldwide depression for the vast majority of people, but also a time when wealthy classes still controlled much of European society. It was not a stretch for some socially minded but privileged individuals at universities to see communism as the superior alternative.

It is important to distinguish initially between the two main types of espionage: human source intelligence (HUMINT) and signals or electronic intelligence (SIGINT). This overview will consider only HUMINT espionage, but it is fair to say that SIGINT successes had far greater impact in a military sense than all the human spy operatives. Just two examples will make this case. The cryptanalytic work that was done by the British at Bletchley Park north of London during World War II had an immeasurable impact on military operations by both the British and American forces throughout the war. The German military code, transmitted through the Enigma Machine, was broken at Bletchley and the secret of the breach was kept by those who knew. As a result, the Germans would continue to use the code unawares until the final days of the war.

Another example was the American code breakers who deciphered the Japanese naval code in 1942, enabling US naval forces to have knowledge ahead of time about Japanese naval operations. These SIGINT methods may to some be less interesting than human operations, and today they are among the most secret activities of technologically advanced countries. Still, HUMINT holds the most compelling and dramatic attraction for millions of readers of both fiction and non-fiction. As mentioned, the 1930s and 1940s were a time when Soviet recruitment of British citizens to spy for the Soviet Union against their own country was unusually successful. The so-called "Cambridge Five" are a classic example of just this point. At Cambridge University in the mid 1930s many students and some faculty were strongly sympathetic to socialism and communism. Four individuals; Kim Philby, Donald Maclean, Guy Burgess, and John Cairncross, were recruited, directly and indirectly, by a faculty member, Anthony Blunt. They left the University and sought positions in the British government in diplomatic and intelligence fields. All were successful and moved up the line to increasingly sensitive positions. They were ideologically committed to the Soviet Union and, for many years, supplied the Soviets with secret intelligence covering different areas, including military and economic planning.

All were eventually uncovered. Maclean and Burgess escaped to Russia in 1953, followed much later by Philby in 1963. Blunt and Cairncross admitted their spying activities but were not prosecuted because they cooperated with British investigators. It was a huge embarrassment to the British intelligence community because of the great length of time it took to discover the "moles" in the system. One reason for this, offered by some observers, is that it was just very difficult for many well-born, highly educated Englishmen to believe their colleagues were traitors.

On the other side, there were virtually no Soviet citizens who were recruited to spy for the British or Americans against their country. However, a few defectors volunteered their services and proved to be extremely useful, especially in identifying Soviet spies in the western country's intelligence services. Two of these defectors were Anatoliy Golitsyn, who identified Philby, and Oleg Gordievsky who fingered Cairncross. There was also Oleg Penkovsky, who was a spy for the British, but who many believe was actually a double agent supplying false information. However, it is clear that he did provide valuable information to the US regarding the Soviet effort to plant missile sites in Cuba. It is safe to say that espionage will always be a part of international competition, but the methods and technology will constantly change. What we actually know about current espionage activities is that they are similar to icebergs: what we see and know is only a fraction of what actually exists.

Chapter 8. European Resistance to Communism

French and Italian Political Resistance

Although the resistance to the military expansion of communism through the establishment of NATO and the American doctrine of containment, both previously discussed, was largely successful, there were other unrelated efforts to elect communist governments by entirely peaceful and democratic means. Two examples of this were the creation of communist political parties in France and Italy. The French Communist Party, known as the PCF *(Parti communiste francais)*, was founded as early as 1920. The PCF had broad support among intellectuals, students, workers, and anti-capitalist liberals. However the Party had limited success in electing officials nationally because of an inability to unify with other likeminded political parties, such as the Socialist Party. There were also divisions within the European communist parties themselves between those, like the PCF, who saw themselves as independent and essentially French, and those communists who were part of the international movement controlled by the Soviet Union. During the 1930s the intellectual support for communism grew rapidly because of the worldwide economic depression. Many people saw communism as a vehicle to protect humane and liberal values. However, World War II changed that for most people. With the power and expansion of the Soviet Union and the establishment of NATO by the Western countries, most governments and political philosophers were forced to choose sides.

The PCF actually reached its zenith in membership with over half a million members in 1946 and received the most votes in the National Assembly elections that year. The PCF initially gained considerable prestige after the war because of their intense resistance to Nazi occupation. There were many observers, including Under-Secretary of State Dean Acheson of the US, who believed that the PCF would soon become the first democratically elected communist government in Europe. But such was not to be the case. The United States imposed severe restrictions regarding access to Marshall Plan assets on governments outside of the Soviet sphere, if those governments were controlled by communist political parties. Because of these restrictions the PCF was forced to withdraw in May of 1947 from the majority French government. Consequently, it grew closer to Moscow and more vociferous against the ruling party in France, calling it the tool of American capitalism.

During the 1950s, the PCF was outside of the French government and largely isolated but remained faithful to the principles of communism. In 1958 the Party opposed the return of Charles de Gaulle to the presidency, but during the following decade they found ways, from time to time, to support him. The PCF was never again a significant force in French politics and, after the brutal response of the Soviets to the Hungarian and Czechoslovak independence demonstrations, the Party moved away from Moscow and identified more with Eurocommunism, an unofficial group of communists not directed by Moscow. After the fall of the Soviet Union in 1991, many European communist parties formally dissolved, but not the PCF. It remained in existence but was marginalized by other left wing groups such as the Socialist Party and the Greens.

The Italian Communist Party, the PCI *(Partito Communista Italiano)*, was always much larger and more influential than its sister the PCF. While both parties were started in the early 1920s, the PCI attained a membership of over two million in 1947. One of the reasons for the success of the communists in Italy was the harsh reaction toward the PCI by Mussolini and the Fascists, who outlawed the Party and persecuted its members. Many PCI members reacted by becoming very active in the resistance against Mussolini and the Nazis. As the war wound down, those fighting the Fascists became very popular among ordinary Italian citizens and communism was seen as far preferable to totalitarian dictatorships.

After the war the PCI was active in helping to write and adopt a democratic constitution and was a major participant in the government, although never part of the majority. These efforts created a political split with the Soviet Union, but the PCI remained connected financially to the Soviets. After the Hungarian revolt in 1956, PCI membership divided almost equally between those who believed the insurgents were counter-revolutionaries who needed to be put down, and those who saw Russia's response as oppressive. Still the Party membership remained impressively large; the US estimated in 1960 that the PCI membership was over 1.3 million, making it the largest communist party in Western Europe. In 1969 the split with the Soviets became, as a practical matter, complete. The Secretary General of the PCI, Enrico Berlinguer, attended a conference of international communist parties in Moscow, and directly told Brezhnev that the suppression of Czechoslovakian reform was a tragedy. He also stated that his Party disagreed fundamentally with the Soviets on such questions as national sovereignty and socialist democracy. During the late 1970s and all of the 1980s, the PCI was definitely affiliated philosophically with Eurocommunism. Consequently, when the Soviet Union and its official connection to communism collapsed in 1991, the dissolution of the PCI was a foregone conclusion.

At mid-century, it seemed quite possible that the political success of the communist movement in Europe might be realized. No two countries exemplified this more than France and Italy. Both had suffered tragically in the war and both were slow to recover economically, creating fertile possibilities for radically different policies. However, the communist parties of both countries were ultimately unsuccessful. One major reason for this, although certainly not the only reason, was the brute efforts at control and the physical oppression used by the Soviets against the eastern European countries within their control.

Greek Civil War

Unlike the French and Italian communist movements, the communists in Greece were initially more inclined to seize power by revolutionary means. The civil war in Greece was essentially a two-phase war. After the Nazi occupation ended in October 1944, a communist-led resistance group established a provisional government which rejected the Greek king and his government-in-exile. The king was supported by the Democratic National Army group and, more importantly, by Britain. The royalist army immediately challenged the communists and fighting broke out. The British intervened and forced a settlement, but it was tenuous at best. Further fighting ensued, but by February 1945 the British had subdued the communists and a general election was held in March. The communists abstained from voting, and consequently a royalist majority was elected. The king was returned to Greece the following year. This ended the first phase of the civil war, but there was much more to come.

The second phase of the war began in March 1946 and lasted until August 1949. The communists, who were known as the EAM-ELAS (which stood for the National Liberation Front) launched a full-scale guerrilla war against the government. Britain was again faced with the international obligation to defend the monarchist government from a take-over by EAM. Of course, by 1946 all of the World War II combatants, including Britain, were demobilizing, and their populations were not at all sympathetic to a new war, no matter where it was located. The British made efforts to encourage de-escalation, or a cease-fire, but the communists recognized the weak military and financial situation of the British and refused to lay down their arms. The British called on the United States to honor the newly declared Truman Doctrine of containment of communism. On March 12, 1947, President Truman asked the US Congress for funding and authority to support the Greek government in their struggle with EAM. This was the first, but not the last, military activity by the US in resisting the spread of communism.

The US did not involve itself in the fighting in Greece but supplied massive amounts of military equipment and important financial backing to the Greek government. A big question in many western minds was what Stalin would do to support the Greek communists. On this point, timing was on the side of the anti-communists. In the late 1940s the Soviet Union was also recovering from a horrendous war and had all it could handle dealing with the occupied areas of Eastern Europe that it controlled. Stalin was still willing to assist political efforts of communist movements, as in France and Italy, but not military wars outside of its sphere of interest.

The Greek Civil War dragged on from mid 1947 to mid 1949, when EAM was finally overwhelmed and most of its members left Greece. For a small country the human suffering was shocking. It is estimated that more than 50,000 people died and over 500,000 were displaced from their homes. This hard won victory over communist forces was solidified by the creation of NATO with Greece as a charter member.

After World War II, the struggle against communism in western and some parts of central Europe was less a contest of competing ideologies than it might have been in the 1930s. The world had seen in vivid contrast the evils of totalitarianism, first from the Nazis and shortly thereafter by the Soviet Union. Democracy and capitalism were viewed by most as the only reasonable alternatives to other forms of government, even if for some this was by default. A ravaged Western Europe had many serious economic and societal problems, but the overwhelming majority of ordinary people craved freedom and an opportunity to prosper.

Chapter 9. The Collapse of the Soviet Union and Modern Russia

The Impact of Mikhail Gorbachev

After Leonid Brezhnev died in 1982, the Soviet Union was virtually leaderless. Two premiers were selected, Iu. Andropov and K.U. Chernenko, who both served a very short time and died within thirteen months of each other. It was clear to most Politburo members that a much younger man needed to be selected. And the obvious choice was Mikhail Gorbachev, who was the next highest member of the Communist Party's Central Committee. Gorbachev, at age 54, was named General Secretary of the Party in 1985, a position tantamount to the leader of the government.

Gorbachev was indeed a major change from all previous Soviet leaders. He was intelligent, well educated, a lawyer, but had spent his entire career as a Communist Party functionary. Although thoroughly committed to Marxism-Leninism, he was respected as open minded and pragmatic. The new premier was the most worldly-wise of any previous Russian leaders and his ability to adjust to unfamiliar situations surprised many foreign leaders. Even his wife, Raisa, was well educated and westernized. The couple made a powerful first impression on many diplomats outside of the USSR.

Probably most important of all, Gorbachev had an understanding of global economics and of the USSR's rapid downward spiral. The ruble had been experiencing double-digit inflation for several years and was essentially rejected in international markets. Due to decades of centralized economic planning and overemphasis on military hardware, many technologies to improve efficiency and productivity had been ignored. This was true across the board from industry to agriculture. Consequently, basic food and consumer products were in short supply, and a ubiquitous black market existed in spite of government efforts to control it.

On the political side, party corruption and general undermining of Soviet authority brought to a head the dramatic collapse of the Soviet Empire. This collapse was greatly accelerated by the accession to power of Gorbachev. In what proved to be the last great attempt to reform the Soviet system, Gorbachev immediately began the most remarkable changes that the Soviet Union had witnessed since the 1920s. Although it was never his intention to destroy either the communist party or the Soviet Union, these reforms loosed forces that, within seven years, would force Gorbachev to retire from office and would end both communist rule and the Soviet Union, as it had existed since the Bolshevik revolution of 1917.

Dynamic leadership was needed to deal with the nation's economic decline and political disarray. Most understood that the country was in trouble and needed to be revitalized. The six years during which Gorbachev was in power were an extraordinarily confusing period. Could communism reform itself, in the process becoming democratic, without abandoning socialism? Or was the rot in the communist regime so deep-rooted that the entire system had to be abandoned before a more efficient and decent order could be created? In 1986 Gorbachev began his move toward the left by adopting a policy of *glasnost,* a vague term that literally means publicity or openness, but that soon acquired a variety of meanings. There was a new tolerance of the distribution of information and opinions on a wide range of issues in Soviet newspapers, journals, and television. Taboo subjects such as Stalinist terror, censorship, degradation of the environment, corruption, and crime began to appear regularly in publications available to all.

Nevertheless, the most pressing problem for Gorbachev was the economy, which continued to deteriorate after he assumed leadership. In the agricultural industry, long the Achilles' heel of the Soviet economy, he replaced many managers and officials, revised production procedures, but retained central control of the collective farms. Unfortunately, he did not encourage private enterprise of small plots to incentivize increased production. Sixty plus years of centralized planning and management was not to be changed over-night. Gorbachev and his economic advisors also realized early on that industrial production would continue to fall behind the West unless advanced technological equipment could be rapidly introduced. The scientific knowledge existed in the Soviet Union in the 1980s to improve commercial technology, but the engineers and financial resources were still being absorbed by the military-industrial sector. The hardliners and the military strongly resisted any serious reallocation of resources.

Gorbachev's inability to revive the economy undermined his other achievements, which were impressive. At no previous time in the history of the USSR did the people enjoy as much freedom as they did in the late 1980s. Although the Soviet Empire had begun to unravel, Gorbachev's skills and his commitment to peaceful reform remained intact. He was thoroughly dedicated to the preservation of the Soviet Union and socialism and made every effort in behalf of both causes. Also important in terms of world peace were the personal relationships that Gorbachev established with two world leaders: President Ronald Reagan of the US and Prime Minister Margaret Thatcher of Britain. He met with Reagan in Geneva in 1985 and again in Reykjavik in 1986. The purpose, particularly of the Reykjavik meeting, was nuclear disarmament and general reductions in military buildup. Both issues were critical to the Soviets because of their deteriorating economic problems and the fact that Reagan, who had recently been reelected, was increasing defense expenditures dramatically. There was also talk of a US Strategic Defense Initiative (SDI) that would develop an intercontinental missile defense system capable of destroying Soviet long -range missiles in flight. If developed, this would have significantly changed whatever remained of the balance of power between the two superpowers. Although they reached no agreement in the 1986 meeting, the two world leaders did sign a nuclear treaty a year later in Washington that required both powers to destroy most ground-based nuclear weapons. All available evidence indicates that this treaty has been honored by both sides.

Gorbachev's policies regarding the Eastern bloc countries were often confused, some believed contradictory. For instance, he allowed significant levels of self-governance over local matters but was firm in opposing any ideological changes that might threaten the communist state. He had previously condemned the Soviet repressions of Hungary and Czechoslovakia but made no moves to encourage any independence or autonomy among the eastern bloc countries. Consequently, beginning in 1989 the countries of the Eastern Bloc--Poland, East Germany, Bulgaria, Rumania, Hungary, and Czechoslovakia-- broke away, declared their independence and discarded communism without encountering any forceful attempt by the Russians to restrain them. The influences and changes that occurred in Poland are illustrative of the powerful feelings of rejection of Soviet occupation in other Eastern Bloc countries.

"Solidarity" was the name of the first Polish trade union that was authorized to exist in the Eastern Bloc without strict control from any communist party. This was done in August of 1980 in order to keep the shipyards operating in Gdansk (previously Danzig). A year later a union leader, Lech Walesa, was elected President of Solidarity. He quickly became an international figure because he expanded the union's demands well beyond labor issues, into peaceful protests for freedom and democracy. Solidarity was firmly supported by the Polish Catholic Church that tied the union's positions to Catholic social teachings. Pope John Paul II reinforced this connection when he visited his homeland of Poland in June of 1983. The Pope was greeted by more than one million Poles in a stadium in Warsaw where he specifically referred with favor to Solidarity. The ruling communist party of Poland was, from that time forward, under an international microscope and in no position to impose repression on the workers of Poland. A few years later, in November of 1989, "The Wall," which had prevented people from moving out of the Soviet sector, began to be dismantled. The Soviet Union as an empire was destroyed forever.

To sum up the six plus years of Mikhail Gorbachev's time as leader of the Soviet Union is not simple because this period in Russian history was as complex as the man himself. It can be argued, as some historians have, that Gorbachev's intentions were honorable and beneficial, such as his policy of glasnost and non-repressive response to the Eastern Bloc countries. His failures are blamed on intense resistance from hardliners at home and the deep malaise created by seemingly impossible economic woes. However, there is another side that must be considered: he never abandoned his faith in Marxism as an economic principle and tried to the end to force reform through a failed concept. Moreover, Gorbachev tried to satisfy both the left and the right of the power structure, usually alienating both. It is certainly clear, though, that Gorbachev instituted changes that would never be reversed and that millions of people in Russia and Eastern Europe are better off today because of them.

Boris Yeltsin, the Disappointing Hero

During the years prior to the ascendancy of Gorbachev to the premiership, he and Boris Yeltsin had been allies and opponents on more than one occasion. Gorbachev tolerated Yeltsin because he saw in him a charismatic leader, particularly in Moscow, who could help to promote the reforms that were necessary. However, Yeltsin angered many Politburo members with his self-promotional style and aggressive anti-corruption efforts. When Gorbachev became General Secretary in 1985 he was persuaded to demote and isolate Yeltsin, but by 1989 Yeltsin had managed, with the help of Gorbachev, to return to an important position as President of the Republic of Russia. Even though Russia was by far the most important Republic, this was clearly a subordinate position to those who held power over the entire Soviet Union.

Yeltsin's golden opportunity came when right wing communist members of the Politburo launched a coup against Gorbachev in August of 1991. He was placed under house arrest at his *dacha* outside of Moscow, but the plotters made several mistakes, the most important of which was not to secure the support of the military. Gorbachev simply returned to Moscow. The coup leaders began to lose their nerve, many disappeared. The army was ordered to surround the Kremlin, which it did, but when ordered to fire on protesters against the coup, the military refused. Yeltsin, who was on the scene, took full advantage in front of live television coverage from all over the world by standing on a tank in Red Square and denouncing the traitors who led the coup.

The attempted take-over failed after three days, but that was not enough to save Gorbachev's government. He did not resign immediately, but Yeltsin, who was now an international hero, made the most of his position as President of the Republic of Russia by proclaiming Russia as independent of the Soviet Union. The vast majority of common Russian citizens applauded this action. The Soviet Union without Russia was, of course, unthinkable, and so the other Soviet republics (Ukraine, Georgia, Armenia, Belarus, Kazakhstan and the other "stans" in Asia) also broke with the mother country. Some were capable of self-reliant independence but others were still dependent on Russia for fuel and other necessities. Relations between the former republics and Russia remain tense and uncertain to this day. How could a superpower empire that had effectively dominated much of Europe for over forty years have collapsed so quickly? Yeltsin offered an explanation: "The world can sigh in relief. The idol of communism, which spread everywhere social strife, animosity, and unparalleled brutality, which instilled fear in humanity, has collapsed."

The enormity and complexity of problems that faced the new, modern Russia after 1991 would have been enough to challenge the most skilled administrator, but clearly that description did not fit Boris Yeltsin. As with his predecessors, Yeltsin's most urgent and difficult problem was the economy. Gorbachev had tried to move from the centrally controlled and publicly owned means of production to what he referred to as, "democratic socialism." However, Yeltsin decided to take the huge step to a completely free market and rapid transfer of government enterprises to private ownership. His economic advisors anticipated that there would be some inflation and devaluation of the ruble, but they were dismayed to see what ensured: within two months of implementation, prices had soared ten times previous levels, the value of the ruble had declined dramatically on the international market, and unemployment had risen rapidly. The lot of the Russian people until 1995 was miserable. Alcoholism, always a problem, increased dramatically, and life expectancy decreased from 75 to 71 for women and from 65 to 58 for men.

The process of privatization of major industries went quickly but was fraught with corruption; ultimately a few very wealthy and powerful individuals controlled large parts of the economy. Obscenely displaying their newly acquired wealth, they were derisively referred to as "the oligarchs." Many also occupied senior positions in the Yeltsin government. Yeltsin, who was never popular with the Politburo, likewise had many enemies in the newly created Parliament. Inevitable struggles between the President and Parliament reached a climax in 1993 when Parliament leaders sought to impeach him. Convinced that he was still popular, Yeltsin arranged a referendum on his policies. Fifty-nine percent of the voters expressed confidence in Yeltsin as President. Failing in this peaceful approach, the Parliament leaders barricaded themselves in the Parliament building, issuing statements deposing Yeltsin and appointing two of their members as Acting President and Defense Minister. Yeltsin ordered dispersal from the building and then surrounded it with loyal army troops. After a few shots were fired, the leaders of the attempted coup surrendered and were eventually convicted and sentenced to prison terms. In a little over two years, Yeltsin had faced down two attempted coups. Unfortunately for Russia, this did nothing to ease economic difficulties.

In 1995 Yeltsin was elected to a second term as President, but the pressures of office and his barely concealed alcoholism were taking their toll on his health. After his five years in office, few had illusions about him. He was seen accurately as impulsive, authoritarian, and isolated. He had no new ideas left but was too stubborn to change any previous policies. However good news was coming: by the second half of the 1990s the economy was improving. Privatization had produced many more consumer goods and available food products than had ever been produced under communism. Corruption was still rampant and too few were benefiting significantly from an improved economy, but many citizens could see a light at the end of the long tunnel.

Yeltsin had serious heart surgery at the end of 1996 and, although he recovered, his energy level, always one of his strengths, was never the same. His political influence declined with his health and lessened activity. By 1998, Russia had defaulted on its international debt obligations and most Russians were envious of their neighbors to the west. Yeltsin acknowledged the obvious and resigned effective on the last day of the century, December 31, 1999. However, even his final act had a profound long-term effect on Russia: he appointed Vladimir Putin to the presidency.

The history of Russia and the Soviet Union is a fascinating study, but no period offers greater extremes and fundamental changes than the 20th century. In little over seventy years Russia's government literally went from a radical left wing, authoritarian, dictatorship to a partially democratic, capitalistic, and largely open society. Major problems remain, and the trend led by Putin appears to be reversing some of the steps forward. Clearly, however, for Russia there will be no returning to anything close to its Byzantine past.

Genocide in Bosnia

Bosnia-Herzegovina is one of the countries that separated from Yugoslavia after the death of Tito in 1980. It is located on the eastern side of the Adriatic and is bordered to the southeast by Serbia. It contains three ethnic groups in roughly equal numbers: Serbs (Orthodox Christians), Croats (Catholics), and Albanians (Muslims). These groups had never lived together in harmony, and during the 1980s there were many episodes of violence and sectarian abuse.

In Serbia, a powerful former communist, Slobodan Milosevic, gained control of the former Yugoslav army and began a campaign of nationalism and religious hatred toward all who were not Serbs and Orthodox Christians. In 1992, Milosevic turned his attention to Bosnia, where the Serb population amounted to approximately 32% and had protested that they were victims of Muslim discrimination and atrocities. There never was compelling evidence to support these claims but that did not stop Milosevic. His army invaded and captured Sarajevo, the Bosnian capital. Sarajevo soon became a killing ground with Serb snipers shooting helpless civilians in the street, eventually killing over 3500 children and an unknown number of adults. The Serbs were particularly cruel to Muslims, using rape against women and girls and murdering men and young boys by the thousands. These atrocities were referred to as "ethnic cleansing."

The United Nations and the US complained, imposed useless economic sanctions, and offered peace conferences, to no avail. However, on February 6, 1994 the world's attention focused on Bosnia when a mortar shell exploded in a market in Sarajevo killing 68 and wounding nearly 200 innocent people. The US, under President Bill Clinton, organized NATO to issue an ultimatum to the Serbs to withdraw their artillery from Sarajevo and comply with a NATO imposed cease-fire. Milosevic and the Serbs responded by taking hundreds of UN peacekeepers hostage and turning them into human shields. Atrocities and genocide continued until finally, in August of 1995, effective military intervention began with a massive US led NATO bombing campaign to drive the Serbs out of Bosnia and to destroy their military infrastructure in Serbia. Muslim-Croat troops occupied Bosnia and Milosevic agreed in November to peace talks in the United States. This ended the first major NATO military operation in the organization's nearly fifty years.

Chapter 10. Rise of the European Community

The Need for Unity

Once reconstruction of the war-torn countries of western Europe had begun, the leadership of some of the largest economies agreed that there was an urgent need for economic unification. This movement started in the early 1950s between France, Germany, and Italy through an association dealing with the production and distribution of coal and steel. The problems that were impeding growth were the cross border restrictions of transportation, tariffs, labor movement, and political concerns. But to many European citizens it was not at all clear why they should get closer together. They spoke different languages, had different traditions and ways of life. It seemed that what separated them was far more important than what they had in common.

Still, other European nations, including many smaller countries in the north, were added but they, from the beginning, were concerned that the larger nations would overwhelm their interests and control the organization to their own benefit. However, the smaller countries, such as Ireland, Austria, the Netherlands, and Portugal, did benefit quite well economically from what was then called the Common Market. These benefits took the form of access to low interest debt for economic development. Another always present issue in the Common Market was the reluctance of most nations to hand over national sovereignty to a central, and virtually anonymous institution over which ordinary people had no control. It was clear some countries had greater influence than others in Brussels, the capital of the Common Market.

Some post war egos and jealousies continued to thwart true unity. In 1963 and again in 1967, Charles de Gaulle, President of France, personally vetoed British efforts to join the union. His stated reason seemed specious to most, that Britain was too closely tied to the US to support the Common Market wholeheartedly. But Britain and many other countries did join in the 1970s so that prior to the collapse of the Soviet Union there were fifteen European members. After the opening of eastern Europe, ten more joined and today there are twenty seven members with several applications pending, including Turkey.

In 1992 an important Treaty was signed by the Common Market members in Maastricht, Netherlands which: created a central bank, established a completely free trade zone, changed the name to the European Union, and set the stage for the introduction in 1999 of a common currency, the Euro. There was great optimism in Europe in the years before the 21st century about a "European Model" that would set the Continent apart from the United States and would be a powerful economic engine moving into the new century. When the 27 countries of the EU are considered as a single trading entity, they do generate the largest Gross Domestic Product (GDP) in the world. Unofficial numbers for 2011 reflect that the EU had a GDP of 17.5 trillion in US dollars with a modest 1.6% growth rate for the year. That compares to the US economy that created a GDP of slightly more than 15 trillion dollars and growth of 2.8%.

But great optimism led to a step too far. The so called European "elite," those financiers, industrialists, and political power brokers who exercised considerable influence over the EU decided that a strong central government with sovereign powers and supported by a constitution was needed. Such a constitution was presented to the membership in 2004 and, to the shock of the elite, it was defeated by large margins in France and the Netherlands. Other countries, including Britain, withheld votes on the constitution which has never been adopted. So the EU is structurally the same today as it was at the turn of the century, but huge financial problems for the eurozone countries currently exist.

Immigration

It became very clear by the mid 1980s that the face and character of Europe was changing demographically. There had always been guest workers and immigrants, but most of them had been European in origin: Italians, Spaniards, Portuguese, and Yugoslavs. But now many new immigrants came from the Middle East, Africa, and Asia. Although some sought political asylum, they had no intention of returning to their homelands.

In the decades before 1980, the movement of people followed three main patterns: the migration from the countryside into the cities; the displacement of virtually entire Jewish populations from eastern Europe and Germany; and decolonization. Although the migration to the cities has slowed somewhat, the percentage of city dwellers in western Europe is approximately 75%. The loss of Jewish populations has deprived Europe of some of it's most vibrant intellectual, religious and cultural life. A third major migration was decolonization, which can be described as the return of Europeans from colonial countries upon those countries achieving independence. While perhaps not true immigration, the impact on countries such as France, which received more than one million returning people from Algeria in 1962, created an overwhelming economic challenge. Similar decolonization was experienced by Britain and the Netherlands.

The impact of these demographic changes, while temporarily negative, did not typically raise the more difficult and long-term problems of lack of assimilation and cultural identity. These problems are at the heart of the massive movement of Middle Eastern, East African, and Asian Muslims into western Europe beginning in the 1980s. Many Muslims had no desire to integrate into European societies the way earlier immigrant waves had done. This resistance to assimilation created increasing social, political, and cultural problems. Thus, overnight what had been considered a relatively minor and local problem was becoming a major political issue with growing resistance on the part of native populations. Perhaps they were wrong to react in this way, but they had not been aware until recently of this trend and no one had ever consulted them. The problems facing west European societies were more often than not the second and third generation immigrants who revolted against their adopted country. The reasons given are poverty, overcrowding, unemployment, and lack of education.

As an example, France is now home to the largest Muslim community in Europe, approximately 5.5 million. This number has doubled since 1980. French policy towards its Muslims has been based on principles of secularism and assimilation. There is the French belief in a homogeneous society with tolerant multiculturalism. Secularism and culture are an impediment to Muslim assimilation because religion has always been an integral part of Muslim identity. Clear evidence of this is the fact that in the mid 1980s there were 260 mosques in France, and today there are over 2,000. So the French model has not worked as well as expected. There were riots in 1994-95 in the French Muslim communities of Northern France and Paris. Although there were indications that the situation in the immigrant community was under control, closer observers noted that the situation was continuing to smolder. By the year 2000, half of the inmates of French prisons were of Muslim origin. There were further riots in November of 2005 and, although religious issues were a factor, most experts estimated that the economy was the major motivating factor.

The German approach to its immigration problem involved well-intentioned people and institutions who promoted integration. These groups included social workers, academic researchers, churches, and political parties. The primary ethnic group immigrating into Germany was Turks who settled mostly in the major German cities such as Berlin, Cologne and Duisburg. They came primarily from the least developed parts of Turkey and were illiterate and far more conservative in their religious beliefs than Turks from Istanbul or Ankara. Thus it came as no surprise that, almost from the moment of their arrival in Germany, Turks confined themselves to their own kind and customs. The Muslim population of Germany today is approximately 3.6 million, of which Turkish immigrants comprise more than half.

While the aim of German policy has been the integration of the Turkish communities, the aim of Islamist organizations, supported by the Turkish government, has been diametrically opposed to integration. The Turks in Germany remain Turks even if they have adopted the German nationality and vote in German elections. There has been some rioting and property destruction in the German Muslim community, but the German economy has been markedly better than other European countries and that is a major reason for less upheaval.

The 1.6 million Muslims in Britain, mainly from Pakistan and Bangladesh, constitute about half of the post-war immigrant population in Britain. According to a variety of polls a majority of British Muslims admitted that they were better treated in the United Kingdom than in any other European countries. There was, for instance, no total legal ban in Britain, in contrast to France and Germany, to wearing the hijab in school or in public. London became the refuge of many extremists who had been sentenced to long prison terms, or even death, in their native countries in the Arab world. Britain also allowed radical organizations, which were banned in many Arab countries such as the Muslim Brotherhood, to operate freely. The attitude of British authorities was traditionally one of benign neglect. As long as the radical Muslim organizations did not commit flagrant breaches of peace, they were left alone. This began to change after the September 11, 2001 terrorist attacks in the United States and the July 7, 2005 underground bombings in London. British authorities took a more active interest in radical preachers who were inciting to murder. Some were deported and others sentenced to prison terms. Today Britain and the US share intelligence information about potential terrorist activities, and it is accurate to say that many planned attacks have been thwarted in both countries. The situation in all western European countries remains volatile with intense homeland law enforcement agencies watching immigrant societies closely.

The Welfare States

The drive for economic security is, psychologists tell us, one of the most important human desires. After World War II, this desire could not have been stronger among the masses of unemployed and impoverished of war- torn Europe. The first European nation to respond to this need was Britain through its Labour Party in the late 1940s and early 50s. Britain created universal health coverage through the National Health Service. The enactment of the law was more an acknowledgement of existing conditions, but it expressed a powerful change in British political opinion. Taxpayer funded health care was a fact of life for all but a few wealthy individuals who could afford the private insurance that was available.

Other countries such as France, Italy, and Germany resurrected political parties that had been popular prior to the war. These parties were often called Christian Democratic parties because most members were active Christians and part of the working class. While there were wide differences of opinion among the members of the Christian Democratic parties on many issues, one subject received unanimous support, lifetime job security and pension guarantees.

One budgetary policy change, made by all western European countries that made it possible to fund increases in social welfare services, was an almost total elimination of defense spending. This was possible because of the creation of NATO and the reliance on the defense capabilities and expenditures of the United States. Generally, substantial economic growth across the west allowed many countries, including Britain, to expand social programs without great strain on their budgets. But by 1980, growth had slowed and even reversed for a time in most regions.

For the British, this resulted in a new government of the Conservative Party with a new Prime Minister, Margaret Thatcher. She was determined to roll back many socialist policies that had been enacted in the last two decades, and to reduce the power of trade unions throughout most industries. Her time in office (1979 to 1990) was marked by constant political battles over budgetary issues, but she and the Conservatives were successful in reversing the trend toward more generous government programs. Thatcher's leadership was gradually followed across the Continent even by left-of-center political parties, like the various Christian Democratic parties of Germany and France.

Many ordinary Europeans resisted reductions in welfare benefits by comparing Europe to the US. This thinking dealt with the concept of the value of leisure time and economic security. The argument was that Europeans valued leisure more than Americans and that as a result, even though poorer, they had a better quality of life. However, many were persuaded that if they remained half as well off as Americans, this would mean poorer health care, education and a diminishment across all kinds of goods and services, and therefore a lower quality of life. There was certainly no broad consensus of opinion. There were those who strongly believed that reforms and cuts in welfare/social benefits had to be made. More and more, frequent questions were asked as to which of the services of the welfare state could be afforded at a time of slow or no growth and a rapidly aging population.

In addition to these problems, there was the long term trend in Europe of an alarming decline in the birthrate. In an article entitled The End of Europe, economist Robert Samuelson drew attention to the discrepancy in birth rates between Europe and America and pointed out that by 2050 one-third of the population of Europe would be 65 or older. Apart from high unemployment and slow growth, how could European economies operate in the future with so many elderly people heavily dependent on government benefits?

As contemporary economists see it, the modern European welfare state redistributed income from the working young to the retired old and from the rich to the poor. As an example, the British welfare state guarantees a minimum standard income and provides social protection in the event of job loss and services at the best level possible. This is the theory. In practice, services are at a low level and have to be rationed according to the funding available. The character of the welfare state varies from country to country. However, all European countries experienced the fact that the welfare state became more and more expensive primarily because people were living longer, medical expenses became much more expensive, and rising unemployment meant fewer jobs producing revenue. Added to that, the number of students had grown five-fold all over Europe since the end of the Second World War. This necessitated more funding for schools and universities and a delay in youth employment to support the welfare state system. Taxes were raised across Europe; in France the overall income tax rate reached 45%.

Economic stagnation at the end of the 20th century caused European higher education and scientific research, once foremost in the world, to steadily decline. All this meant a further reduction in Europe's position in the world and, at the same time, less defense spending weakened its ability to be a military partner of the United States or even to project military power for peacekeeping purposes.

Chapter 11. The United States Emerges

Governance

It can be said that, after the Great War and the decisions taken at Paris, America entered the new decade as the most important world power, but did so kicking and screaming. As the least impacted, in every important way of the principal combatants, many in America simply wanted to get on with business and life generally without the impediment of European controversies. The isolationist views of a majority in Congress, and probably a majority of the public, were made abundantly clear when the Senate rejected the League Treaty by a large margin and the Country moved on to domestic issues. However, because the political atmosphere of the US had become stagnant, that did not mean that there was no other energy or progress in other fields. Indeed, the economic growth that occurred in the decade of the 1920s was without precedent.

The Progressive period, usually associated with Woodrow Wilson, had clearly run its course by the spring of 1920 with the rejection of US membership in the League of Nations and with serious health problems afflicting Wilson. Although the Democrats tried to continue the Wilsonian progressivism by nominating the reform Governor of Ohio, James M. Cox for President, and Franklin Roosevelt, the promising Assistant Secretary of the Navy as Vice President, the Country was already looking inward and wanted no more foreign or domestic adventures. The Republicans nominated a virtually unknown but non-controversial Senator from Ohio, Warren G. Harding, with Calvin Coolidge standing for Vice President. Harding promised a return to "normalcy" and aggressive business growth. Apparently, this suited the electorate because he won easily, even though he admitted privately that he was ill suited for the job. Most historians agree that Harding was probably the least prepared of all Presidents from the aspects of experience, temperament, and vision.

Hiram Johnson, a Progressive Governor of California, summed up the negative viewpoint of the Progressives, who were a liberal wing of the Democratic Party, very well. "The war has set back the people for a generation. They have bowed to a hundred repressed acts. They have become slaves to the government. They are frightened at the excesses in Russia. They are docile; and they will not recover from being so for many years. The interests that control the Republican Party will make the most of their docility."

After Harding died in August of 1923, he left a short history of little accomplishment, but some scandal. He was succeeded by Calvin Coolidge who had had better experience as Governor of Massachusetts, but who also had a bland personality and a strong resistance to "government interference with business." He famously said, "The business of the American people is business." Indeed, the American people might be excused for not noticing the change in Presidents since neither seemed intent on exercising the powers of the office in any way other than as strictly necessary. Consequently, the void in governance was filled by the conservative Congress and their powerful allies, major corporations. Even the Supreme Court, lead by Chief Justice William Howard Taft, resisted many attempts to use the regulatory power of the government to alleviate business abuse. So it is fair to say that business interests largely controlled, or at least heavily influenced, the operations and decisions of the Federal Government during the 1920s. "Never before, here or anywhere else, has government been so completely fused with business" opined the *Wall Street Journal.*

The Economy

The dramatic increase in the American economy during the first half of the decade may have been due to, as many argued at the time and some continue to argue long after, this *laissez faire* approach to business. Private sector manufacturing and industrial production in America experienced an unprecedented period of development during the decade of the 1920s. The principal European countries, that were natural competitors of the US for commercial goods, were left economically devastated by the Great War, while the US was untouched physically and only briefly affected financially. Thus, American businesses had a steady source of demand for their goods – literally as fast as they could be produced. Rapid and efficient production processes became the all important pathway to huge profits. The other indispensible life-blood of business besides demand, and the ability to meet it, is the financing required to improve and expand manufacturing facilities. Again, the US stood alone in the industrial world as the financer with the greatest available resources to invest in and loan to expanding businesses. These advantages, plus a ready and available workforce, placed the US in an unchallengeable position economically.

Production nearly doubled in the decade and in no other industry is this better illustrated than the automobile industry. Almost 4,300,000 cars rolled off production lines of Ford and its competitors, General Motors and Chrysler, in 1926. Related development, such as highway expansion and improvement and emergence of suburbs, also grew at an amazing pace. Public investment in these and other industries, as reflected in stock prices, increased in a seemingly unending upward spiral.

American homes became the envy of the world, not only because of their size, but also because of the many new electric conveniences; toasters, irons, vacuum cleaners, stoves and refrigerators. For the first time, virtually all of the public could enjoy, at very little cost, entertainment through ready access to radio and talking motion pictures. Many new, non-industrial jobs in white-collar positions such as sales, advertising, and clerical, were filled with people who had never had opportunities to be in those positions before.

However, these internal changes in American society were only a part of a much larger and complex world economy that benefited the US immensely. As mentioned, all the major Western European economies were in economic depression, none worse than Germany. To its credit, the American government realized that a massive and realistic loan program for all of the weak economies needed to be created. As stated by Secretary of State, Charles Evans Hughes, this program was not just for humanitarian purposes but also in the self-interest of the US economy. The Dawes Plan, as it was known, was adopted in 1924 and made loans available to European governments, especially Germany, for trade and economic development. (Charles Dawes was Harding's budget director and later Vice President under Coolidge). The US contributed 55%, or $105,000,000, to the fund. America thus became the largest creditor nation in the world, a position it held until fairly recently. The loans required the debtor nations to buy American goods in most cases, and even to transport their imports on American vessels where available. The economic recovery in Europe was uneven with Britain and France recovering by mid decade, but German industry taking nearly the full ten years to return to pre war levels. So the US was in a powerful position economically and in terms of governmental stability *viv-a-vis* other industrial nations. But all was not well because intolerance, bigotry, and fear mongering rose once again in many American societies.

The Red Scare, Immigration, and the Ku Klux Klan

By 1920, Bolshevism and Vladimir Lenin were entrenched in Russia and the capitalist world was watching with increasing concern that this communist ideology would, as Marx predicted, spread to the democracies. Many feared that organized labor would be the pathway to communism. Union labor in the US was dominated by the American Federation of Labor (AFL) and its charismatic leader, Samuel Gompers. The AFL tried from the beginning to clarify in the minds of the public that it was staunchly opposed to the principles of communism. The AFL had always worked within the framework of the existing economic order and was a firm supporter of the capitalist system. However, other labor unions such as those representing textile workers, mine workers, and railroad workers held a variety of views running from socialist demands to corporate power sharing ideas. But all unions firmly protected their ultimate bargaining power - the strike.

Gompers and the leadership of the AFL were essentially conservative and had enjoyed great union growth and prosperity during the tremendous industrial production of the war years. Consequently, Gompers moved promptly against these "radical" influences gaining hold within the labor movement. In making this attack on labor radicalism, AFL union officials were always careful to emphasize the fact that organized labor as a whole was not tainted by this extremism. So while there were labor strikes from time to time in various industries, labor unrest never became the threat to government or business in the US as was commonly experienced in Europe during the decade of the 1920s.

In 1921 President Harding signed the Emergency Quotas Act, which greatly restricted immigration into the US. The law set a new ceiling of 357,000 total immigrants per year and a quota for each nationality equivalent to 3% of its population in the US, based on the 1910 census. This was a significant reduction from prior years, but the most dramatic impact was the discriminatory effect it had on Asian and East European nationalities whose populations in 1910 were much smaller than white, Anglo-Saxon Americans. The drive to slow immigration was often called "Americanization," which meant to many the adoption of the language, social customs, and political values of WASP America.

Claims were made by some, that Catholic immigrants owed primary allegiance to the Vatican, Italian immigrants rejected the Protestant work ethic in favor of criminal activities, and Jewish communities were engaged in conspiracies to control the nation's money supplies. One prominent propagator of anti-Semitic views was Henry Ford, who alleged Jewish plots to monopolize certain markets and financial institutions. In spite of the patent discrimination of these assertions, the Quotas Act was very effective. From June 1920 to June 1921, 805,228 immigrants were admitted but after the law became effective, the annual total fell sharply to 309,556.

The Ku Klux Klan experienced an increase in membership in about 1915 with its apogee in 1925. Many Americans perhaps thought that the Klan was a 19th Century abomination whose time was long past, but racial and religious hatred rose after World War I and found a receptive home in the Klan. Those bigoted against blacks, Catholics, Jews, and urban liberals could nurture their ignorance and hatred with like-minded individuals. Unlike the phenomenon of the prior century when the KKK was confined primarily to the south, the growth in the 1920s was fueled by nativist hostility to Catholic, Asian, and Jewish immigrants, as well as the movement of huge numbers of blacks from the south to the cities in the north. Klan propaganda spread lies and fear in WASP communities against moral degradation, bootlegging, prostitution, political corruption, gambling, and even jazz. In Indiana, both the Klan and the Anti-Saloon League were politically powerful and Klansmen were able to set up a national headquarters there. Although Klan influence was still strongest in rural areas and small communities, they were able to elect a Klan member as Governor of Oregon, as well as public officials in the cities of Denver, Los Angeles and Chicago.

The Military

With virtually all nations significantly reducing their military budgets in the immediate years after World War I, and with no real formulas established by the Versailles Treaty to guide rearmament, President Harding offered an opportunity to Britain, Japan, France, and Italy to confer with the US in Washington on setting limits for naval and all other military rebuilding. Harding was perhaps not adverse to demonstrating that the League of Nations, which he had opposed, was not the only international body capable of planning peaceful objectives. The five nations began discussions in November of 1921 in what was simply called the Washington Conference. Belgium, the Netherlands, Portugal, and China also accepted invitations as essentially observer participants. Limitations on the tonnage of warships quickly became the focus of negotiations. This was so because of a nearly universal belief by military strategists that world powers would, for the foreseeable future, be impacted by the ability to move about and control the sea-lanes in Europe and beyond. Also controlling this aspect of military rearmament was far easier to accomplish than controlling the rebuilding of land armies. It is impossible to conceal major warships on the high seas of the world.

The US, Japan, Britain, France, and Italy signed a Five-Power Treaty in February of 1922 which established the following naval tonnages:

	US	Britain	Japan	France	Italy
Capital ships	525,000	525,000	315,000	175,000	175,000
Aircraft carriers	135,000	135,000	81,000	60,000	60,000

Although aircraft carriers were a relatively new concept, and certainly not embraced by a majority of admirals around the world, enough far-sighted naval strategists correctly saw their potential and were aggressively arguing for aircraft carrier construction. This was especially true in the US and Japan.

There was also an agreement between America, Britain, and Japan to scrap huge tonnages of old vessels, and not to refit them. The British and Japanese delegations resisted this US initiative but, in the end, signed the Agreement. This is one powerful example of the emergence of US influence in international matters. The Five-Power Treaty was widely accepted by the governments of

Britain, France, and Italy because they were anxious to avoid placing extra pressures on their struggling economies.

The great irony of the success of the Washington Conference is that President Harding, who had opposed US membership in the League, had, in his first year in office, achieved what was universally regarded as a historic event in which, for the first time, the major powers had agreed to restrain armament production, at least in naval terms. Of course, in less than a decade, many of these major powers were again involved in a competitive arms race leading to another world war. The whole American effort to reduce and limit future arms production was, nevertheless, an important development in post-war American foreign policy – led by an isolationist.

Industrial and Military Innovation

After a brief economic recession from 1920 to 21, the American industrial sector recovered quickly. It was the envy of the industrialized world because it became the first economy geared to the production of consumer goods and leisure related fare for the masses. This new economy was sometimes referred to as "people's capitalism" because profits were achieved by high volume production, resulting in much greater abundance than had ever been experienced before. America had indeed learned how to build a technically advanced economy that was far more efficient and also attuned to popular desires and needs.

From 1922 to 1928 the index of industrial production rose 70% and unemployment largely disappeared. Efficiency was at the heart of these advances as illustrated by the fact that output per factory worker-hour climbed nearly 75%. However, one important sector, agriculture, did not share in the expansion and profitability of other industries. This was not due to lack of technological improvements; indeed far better tractors, trucks, and other farm equipment was produced to efficiently increase the supply of agricultural products. But that was the great irony. American food production had exceeded domestic consumption for several years, but the excess products found ready markets abroad. This changed drastically, in Europe especially, after the war because most European countries were spending scarce resources to reinvigorate their own agricultural economies. With the decline in export markets and over-production at home, food prices fell to the point that farmers could not make a profit. The more they produced, the less profit they made.

To fuel technological innovations in industry, new and less expensive power sources, besides steam and oil burning engines, were needed. Electricity had been the answer for most industries for at least twenty years, but access to electric power was limited in most of the rural and western parts of the country. Power companies all over America raced to extend electric lines that were relatively inexpensive to construct. By the end of the decade more than half of the nation's industries were using electricity, and 63% of residences were wired. This development was much faster and more extensive than other industrial nations were able to generate.

In the field of medicine, important discoveries were made by American and European scientists, such as, the research leading to the use of insulin for diabetics and vitamins E, A, and D for various dietetic disorders. Unrelated to medicine but no less important to future American endeavors, was the successful use of liquid fuel to propel long-range rockets. Robert Goddard's rockets in 1926 marked the first step in the expansion of the human range beyond the atmosphere.

In the military-scientific arena, the US was also taking giant steps forward. Advances in aircraft design and power moved from the bi-wing planes of World War I to single wing and duel engine planes that could fly at much higher altitudes and go much greater distances. Technical improvements were advancing in parallel between Europe and America, but the US was able to produce far more airplanes than European countries because of its stronger economy. Also the vast, open spaces of America's west created commercial opportunities for aircraft use, such as: crop dusting, postal delivery, and the very popular stunt flying shows. The most famous aircraft demonstration, of course, was the first successful, solo pilot, non-stop flight across the Atlantic completed by Charles Lindbergh in May of 1927. The 25 year old pilot had flown from New York to Paris in 33 1/2 hours and became an instant sensation on both sides of the ocean. The flight of "Lucky Lindy" convinced many Americans that air travel was the wave of the future.

Although the military in the US was not producing large numbers of airplanes, the scientific and engineering developments necessary to produce modern aircraft were being completed and tested for future use. Possibly, the single most important military development was the practical use of aircraft carriers. As early as 1923, the US military demonstrated that light bombers could take off from carriers and attack both land based and naval targets successfully. The first demonstrations did not include the ability to retrieve aircraft on the carrier, but this important aspect was accomplished very soon afterward. The US led the world in naval aircraft carrier construction and tactical deployment. However, Japan followed this "radical" thinking with its own aggressive airplane and carrier deployments. In the 1920s, most naval planners still relied primarily on battleships, submarines, and fast surface ships to control the sea lines necessary to protect their countries. But after the end of the decade, aircraft carriers were permanently integrated into the naval forces of the US and Japan.

Society and Culture

In looking back nearly 100 years to the 1920s in the United States, one conclusion is inescapable. There were extremes, both positive and negative, in the makeup of American society and culture. It was a period of amazing energy and societal change. The country became urbanized for the first time. Old lifestyle patterns were being discarded by many young and middle-aged people, but these changes were not universally accepted, particularly in the rural small towns and in the south. Prior to the 1920s, white classes, who had immigrated from Northern European countries, were decidedly in the majority. They believed in hard work, thrift, sobriety, and individual initiative. They disliked personal indulgence, diversity, and generally, the vibrant lifestyles of the big cities. In short, the "good old days" were being threatened by city-bred vices.

Few things illustrated the widening gap in society better than the adoption in 1919 of the Eighteenth Amendment to the Constitution – Prohibition. Support for the Amendment came principally from conservative religious organizations, powerful "dry" political groups usually led by women, and by politicians who were fearful of the new women's vote that came into effect in 1920. Enforcement of the Prohibition law was inconsistent in the early years, but by 1925 an unspoken balance had been struck that allowed prohibitionist ideals to be recognized and accepted by those who wished to do so, while a tolerance toward law breaking and even bootlegging was given a blind eye. A repeal movement was beginning in 1925 led by urban Democrats and wealthy businessmen who argued that Prohibition was not progressive reform but rather a denial of cultural and individual freedom, as well as a breeder of crime and corruption. Indeed the criminal element in every major city had experienced a bonanza with a virtual monopoly of supply to an insatiable demand for alcohol. The gang warfare over control of supply and regions was violent and seemingly unstoppable. Some city governments, such as in New York, Detroit, and Chicago, were also tied in to the criminal activities, and enforcement of the law was essentially non-existent. Although federal authorities, led by the FBI, made dramatic and highly publicized attacks on the mob, the criminal involvement in illegal alcohol did not cease until Prohibition was abolished with the adoption of the 21st Amendment in 1933.

On a far more positive note, the nation's public educational institutions were being transformed in many important ways. First of all, enrollments in colleges and universities nearly doubled from 598,000 in 1920 to 1,101,000 in 1930. The causes of this increase were many, but perhaps the most important cause was the widespread view that higher education was valuable and a necessary step in upward mobility. Teachers were being required to meet higher professional standards and to adopt newer methods. In many parts of the country, traditional goals of education were being expanded to include social, technical, and intellectual skills needed for a globally leading nation. Public institutions of higher learning were, for the first time, competing for the best students on a nearly equal basis with the elite private schools.

The increase in leisure time also contributed to the expansion of typically American sports like baseball and football from the college campuses to the professional fields. The New York Yankees and the St. Louis Cardinals drew record crowds and profited millions for their owners. Names like Babe Ruth, Lou Gehrig, and Rogers Hornsby became better known to the general population than major political figures. In football, the Chicago Bears, with their superstar "Red" Grange, and the New York Giants, built huge stadiums and regularly attracted crowds of up to 100,000. Professional boxing emerged, at least partially, from the shadows of corruption with true champions like Jack Dempsey and Gene Tunney. All of these new, successful sports, with their heroes, gave some American people feelings of national pride bordering on attitudes of superiority.

Culturally, America was creating its own, unique artistic pursuits that were, at the same time, separated from European models, and also a part of the centuries long cultural leadership of Europe. The American novel is one of the best examples of this point. It was largely developed from a group of young writers whose styles were fresh and pointed, using short, strong words and sentences, often filled with satire and sarcasm. F. Scott Fitzgerald, Ernest Hemingway, Sinclair Lewis, and Theodore Dreiser exemplified this uniquely American prose. They wrote of individuals destroyed in different ways by the war experience, and of the hypocrisy of degenerate elites and pleasure seekers. Fitzgerald's *The Great Gatsby* is considered by many to be the best of this genre and truly a great American novel. Still, for all their new styles and themes, American writers were clearly based in the traditional strictures of the English language, inherited from centuries of classical English literature.

Another great example of uniquely American culture created during the 1920s is jazz. Jazz music was born in New Orleans among Creole blacks but it spread quickly to Chicago and many points north. It was so popular that the period became known as the "Jazz Age." This new form of music took the country by storm in the decade and was admired by the general public and serious music critics alike. Jelly Roll Morton was an early jazz composer and innovative pianist who influenced virtually all jazz entertainers who followed. The most famous and internationally popular performer, however, was Louis Armstrong whose tours of Europe later earned him the nickname of the "Ambassador." These, and many other leisure time activities, were spread across the country through the expansion of the radio, which was inexpensive and present in most every home.

In conclusion, it is fair to say, that of all the countries considered here during this critical decade, the United States changed most dramatically and positively. But amazing and fearful changes were also occurring in Eastern Europe.

Chapter 12. Russia Becomes the Soviet Union

Governance

No country experienced as much turmoil and change after the war as Russia, but by 1921 Vladimir Lenin and the Bolsheviks had achieved control over all the immense Russian territory, except the rural east and northeast. After 400 years of autocratic monarchies, virtually all Russians were ready for drastic changes in the operation of government. The peasants and ordinary workers wanted a measure of economic security and, for most, this meant some form of property ownership. The Marxist philosophy of the Bolsheviks that proclaimed the control of all property by the state through soviets or councils of workers, certainly sounded like a huge improvement over the serfdom of the past. Lenin, the supreme leader until his death in 1924, was certainly aware of the people's desires but he had the very urgent need to move the economy forward quickly and by any means necessary.

So to understand the basic qualities making up the governance of the Soviet Union at its birth, it is necessary to have a clear picture of Vladimir Lenin, the man and the zealot. A splendid description comes from a contemporary western journalist, Paul Scheffer, who was present at an important speech given by Lenin, submitting an accounting of his government for the year 1921. This occurred in Moscow on December 25, 1922 and is colorfully described by Scheffer.

> From his first sentence I could sense the practiced speaker, who, however, warms to his task slowly. He must have delivered a hundred words before he lifted his eyes for a first glance at the audience before him...There was no effort, even, to persuade. One sensed a hard inflexible will that filled every atom of the man. He told where he stood, and where others stood; and those others were then tossed aside with harsh thrusts of scorn, by deadly shafts barbed with wit.

But even the Marxist zealot, Lenin, was forced to compromise, at least temporarily, his long held beliefs to resurrect a moribund and declining economy.

The Economy

The economic calamities that faced the Soviet leaders in the early years of the 1920s seemed insurmountable, and would have been a severe challenge regardless of the type of government that existed. Industrial production in 1920 had declined to 13 per cent of its prewar volume and peasant land seizures had significantly reduced governmental grain requisitions leading to famine across the country. Starvation was a real threat to an estimated 25 million Russians. Cholera, typhus, and mental panic leading to many suicides was perhaps the most obstinate and incurable of the effects of the whole tragedy.

Lenin's New Economic Policy (NEP) brought some relief, especially in agricultural production, because it opened up a free market to the peasants for their production, and uncontrolled trade between town and country was encouraged. A state bank that exercised control over all banks was created, and the value of the ruble was tightly controlled. Still industrial production lagged other improvements and consumer products were virtually ignored.

A surprisingly candid report on the achievements of Soviet industries was provided about a decade later by the government that said, in part:

> Russian industry is advancing unevenly, joltingly, dispropor-
> tionately. In spite of the existence of a plan, badly needed coal mines
> are opened and operated slowly. At the same time, gigantic plants
> are erected when there is no immediate need for their products.
> ... transportation remains at pre-Soviet levels. New plants are
> equipped with machinery and apparatus which the workers are
> not qualified to handle either by education or technical training.

Expressing an amazing (to western minds) lack of concern for its native population, the report goes on to say:

> Because of its monopoly of foreign trade, Russia is protected
> from any competition of foreign goods...Holding in its hands all
> production and all export trade, the Soviet government fixes two
> sets of prices for its products: a high one for the internal market
> and a low one for the foreign.

It is clear from this official report, that even in the 1930s, the Soviets were still trapped in their economic beliefs that total centralized control of all aspects of production was necessary, and with no appreciation for the benefits of private enterprise.

In 1928, Stalin introduced the first of three Five Year Plans. This Plan was more than an economic scheme but actually inaugurated a new phase in Russian history in which government fiat invaded every aspect of life in such a complete manner as to be unprecedented, not only in Russia, but in any other country at that time. The Plan, as devised by Stalin, shows that his motivation was ideological as much as it was a plan for the economy. He was determined to abolish private ownership of property and to turn the entire population into employees of the state, and thereby dependent on the state. This single-minded purpose was the brainchild of one man who was determined to follow its directives regardless of the toll on human beings.

Arts, Culture and Religion

It is easy for those of us in the west to view the sphere of culture and the arts in Soviet Russia through the lens of the oppressive 1930s and 1940s. Such, however, was not the case in the 1920s. While there certainly was a new interest in, and zeal for, the proletarian and workers new role in society, there was no official suppression of the arts. Writers, composers, and artists in the classical style continued to work and produce significant contributions to the already rich history of Russian culture. Official Soviet Russia was consumed with other major challenges such as counter-revolutionaries, a depressed economy, and internal rivalries for power. The most that the government did in the 1920s in the cultural arts area was to promote (and pay for) poetry, songs, and pedestrian plays that glorified the workers and the imagined egalitarian society.

There were serious writers who went along with the regime, but eschewed the ideology associated with it. Trotsky referred to them as, "poputchika" (fellow travelers). Many literary figures found openings for their essays in the very popular monthly journal *Red Virgin Soil*, edited by A.A. Voronsky. Voronsky was an intellectual who supported Marxism but who freely criticized some aspects of the overall philosophy. He believed, like Trotsky, that art had its own "peculiar laws" in opposition to militant conformists who believed that art should merely reflect life mechanically. *Red Virgin Soil*, and other literary publications, gave protection and some financial help to writers of many points of view. Trotsky supported them while other officials merely tolerated their work.

By the middle of the 1920s, the fellow travelers were free to write, publish and travel outside the USSR. Some *émigré* writers even returned, if only briefly, from places like Berlin, Paris, and Prague. All of this freedom was, however, subject to self-imposed restraint when it came to outright criticism of the government or its officials. On the whole, most Russians could see slow but steady improvement in their living conditions and credited the policies of the NEP. They were not open to much criticism of the government.

Still some astute observers were beginning to see dark clouds on the cultural horizon. The western journalist previously mentioned, Paul Scheffer, describes a scene in Moscow in September of 1928:

> ...eighty persons from many parts of the world...were pilgrims to the Tolstoy memorial celebration. Many of them were foreigners who could hardly have been aware what a remarkable thing, in this land torn by the struggles of Communist thought, such a pilgrimage to the tomb of the one Christian prophet, the one true evangelist of our day, had to be...But in this realm of a new Gospel, a gospel that tolerates nothing which does not echo its own Word, the medal of that gentle, that mighty zealot, has to be recast. Tolstoy and Communism! What different things! What contrary things!

But for a time at least, the same atmosphere existed in the other arts. The great film maker Sergei Eisenstein produced *Potemkin* which dramatized the real mutiny aboard the Battleship Potemkin in 1905. The film received worldwide acclaim for its political statement against Tsarist cruelty. Also young composers, such as Sergei Prokofiev and Dmitry Shostakovich, were creating some of their greatest works. Primarily because of economic conditions in the USSR, these compositions were often heard first and received great praise in the west. However, by the end of the decade, Stalin had consolidated his power and he rapidly embarked upon an anti-intellectual campaign to control the arts to his own narrow and unimaginative preferences.

The relationship of the Soviet government to religion, and to the Russian Orthodox Church specifically, was not so tolerant as it was toward the arts. Lenin expressed his views on the subject of religion as early as 1905: "Religion teaches those who toil in poverty all their lives to be resigned and patient in this world, and consoles them with the hope of reward in heaven. As for those who live upon the labor of others, religion teaches them to be charitable in earthly life, thus providing a cheap justification for their whole exploiting existence... Religion is the opium of the people."

The Bolshevik government, from the very beginning, confiscated buildings and other valuable property of the churches to help finance the Revolution. Most of the smaller religious organizations went underground or dispersed from the urban areas to the country. The Russian Orthodox Church was permitted to continue performance of its rites, but no more. Its schools were closed and some of its largest buildings were converted into museums to glorify Soviet workers. But on the whole, it appears that the government was very cautious in its dealings with the Church. Lenin, as much as he professed to despise ecclesiastic authority, could not afford to antagonize the Orthodox Church and its Patriarch. By the end of the decade, however, Stalin was in a much stronger position generally. To have any hope of improving one's status in Communist society, it was necessary to accept the atheistic dogma rigidly expected of members of the party. The Russian intelligentsia had in large part defected from Orthodox Christianity before the Revolution, so it was essentially the peasants and urban poor who remained consistent churchgoers. Thus church activities declined precipitously.

The Soviet Union of the 1920s was, arguably, the most changed of all developed countries, but its future was far from certain. Its government was totally authoritarian, its economy was in shambles but improving, and its international relations were secretive and threatening. The capitalist west, particularly after Stalin seized power, viewed with growing alarm Soviet efforts to convert other countries to socialist/communist economic practices. The USSR, because of its size, huge population, and abundant natural resources, was certainly a country to be watched carefully.

Chapter 13. German Recovery

Governance

The German economic recovery in the 1920s was nothing short of astonishing, especially considering the fact that the country was coming from a far more depressed condition than any other European country. Unfortunately, for long-term progress, the same could not be said for the governance of Germany in the decade. The Weimar Republic, which was the unofficial name given to the German Reich, was established in Weimar, Germany after the former government dissolved and the Kaiser left the Country on November 9, 1918. A national assembly was convened in Weimar and a new constitution was written. The Republic was to be governed by a president and the Reichstag. The president would be elected every seven years, would manage all foreign affairs, and would appoint civil and military officers, including a chancellor. He was the supreme commander of the armed forces and he alone convened and dissolved the Reichstag. The most notorious clause in the constitution dealing with presidential powers provided that, in an emergency, the president could suspend civil liberties and take whatever steps he deemed necessary to restore law and order. The thinking at the time was that with the many threats from the right and the left to take over the government by force, a strong executive with adequate authority was necessary to preserve peace and rebuild the economy.

Legislative authority was given to the Reichstag, which held elections every four years. Their members came from regions of roughly equal population but also representative of Prussian historical significance. This was done to give a voice to the smaller districts and to ensure that political divisions would be faithfully represented in the Reichstag. The actual effect of this system was to unnecessarily complicate and delay the legislative process, which then caused the president or chancellor to act ahead of legislative approval. The combination of a powerful executive and a relatively weak legislature made it much easier later for Hitler to assume dictatorial powers without the need to change existing constitutional laws.

The extremes of the right and the left groups in society shared at least one important belief: a lack of commitment to democracy. For a nation less than a century old, and with very little past experience in the democratic process, this is hardly surprising. One still very influential part of German society that successfully resisted democratization was the army. The resurgence of the German army in both military might and prestige was primarily due to the uncompromising efforts of one man, Hans von Seeckt, a gifted Prussian officer who was appointed over-all commander in 1920. He had one object in life, the restoration of military power and he pursued that goal tenaciously for six years. However, he also believed that the state owed allegiance to the military and not the other way around. He correctly stated, for the current times in Germany, that the government could not exist without the support of the army. His interest in democracy was lukewarm at best.

So it was clear to any objective observer that totalitarian authority, in alliance with the military, was a strong probability in the near future unless economic conditions improved and moderate leaders arose to guide the country in a different direction. Such a leader did arise for a brief time, Paul von Hindenburg, a revered, retired Field Marshall of the army. However, well before Hindenburg came out of retirement in 1925, the newly established Weimar Republic had to deal with the Allies in the "settlement" of war claims.

Disappointment with the Treaty of Versailles

The representatives of the Weimar government were the unfortunate individuals who had to receive the bad news. Germany was deliberately left out of all of the discussions at Paris and their officials were summoned in June of 1919 to formally accept the terms of the Treaty as a *fait accompli*. The territorial provisions of the Treaty were harsh, but in some respects, expected. For instance, Alsace-Lorraine was restored to France and the Rhineland, that area west of the Rhine River and historically part of Germany, remained German but was declared a demilitarized zone under foreign military control. Because of the destruction of French coal mines by retreating German armies, the German mines in the Saar area near Alsace-Lorraine were provided to France to exploit coal for an indeterminate period. Adjustments were made in Belgium's favor regarding the border area with Germany. In east Germany, the most severe in German estimation, territorial losses involved the Polish corridor. Poland was reinstated as an independent nation with land losses from Germany, Russia, and Austria. The historically Prussian city of Danzig, with an overwhelming German speaking population, became an international city, giving Poland access to the Baltic and controlled by the League of Nations. There were other territorial losses including virtually all German colonies in Africa.

But that was far from all of the recriminations imposed by the leaders of the "victorious" nations. The payment of reparations was a particularly offensive requirement because it went beyond just destruction of territory by the German armies, but was intended as a punishment to Germany for having started the war. In spite of overwhelming evidence to the contrary, the German people did not believe that their Kaiser had precipitated the beginning of the war. The reparations were set at five billion dollars per year for five years with a later sum to be determined by the Allies. In fact, no such exorbitant funds were ever paid, or could have been paid by Germany. Finally, there was the very justifiable issue of restrictions on German rearmament. France was the leader among the Big Three in insisting on almost total limitations on German military rearmament. The military was required to surrender or destroy all heavy weapons and dismantle their naval base at Heligoland. The army could have no more than 100,000 men and they were to have no tanks, poison gas, or aircraft. The Navy would have no more than 15,000 sailors, no capital ships or submarines, and only small coastal defense vessels.

However, as early as 1920 when Seeckt was appointed to head the rebuilding of the military, that effort began in earnest. At first the rebuilding program was in compliance with the terms of the Treaty, but within a few years a secret rearmament movement was underway. Seeckt stated his military plans clearly and simply, "The whole future of warfare appears to me to be in the employment of mobile armies, relatively small but of high quality, and rendered distinctly more effective by the addition of aircraft." This could be a fair description of the *blitzkrieg* employed later by Hitler's *Wehrmacht*.

In furtherance of his military rebuilding goals, Seeckt entered into secret discussions with the Bolsheviks to build Junker airplanes, tanks, poison gas products, and 300,000 artillery shells in exchange for money and training from German officers in the use of the most modern equipment. Seeckt and his counterparts in Russia seemed not to care about the potential in future years of mutual aggression. Winston Churchill, who most probably did not know about the secret agreements, but who sensed a growing rapprochement between the two countries, described it as, "a comradeship of misfortune."

The Economy

From the German point of view, the French and Belgian occupation of the Ruhr Valley coalfields was a devastating blow to their economic recovery. The exploitation of coal began on January 11, 1923 in response to the complete failure by Germany to pay the required reparations. The German coal industry was one of the few major industries functioning at near pre-war levels and necessary for domestic consumption as well as a small but growing export activity. Britain and the US opposed this further step by France and Belgium, but it is fair to say that all three countries involved were still suffering economically in the early 1920s. The Germans reacted by claiming that France had violated the terms of the Versailles Treaty and that the real French purpose was to continue Germany indefinitely as a second rate economy.

The Ruhr occupation was the last straw for the German economy that was virtually paralyzed by uncontrollable inflation. Early in 1923, the dollar was worth approximately 18,000 marks, and by August it was worth roughly 4,600,000 marks. The mark's value declined even more but as a practical matter the German currency was worthless. Gustav Stresemann was appointed chancellor in August of 1923, and although he only served in this capacity for nine months, he restored the economy with several prompt but risky actions. Within three days he established a bank, called the *rentenbank*, and a new mark, referred to as a *rentenmark*. The value of the rentenmark was supported by a mortgage on all industrial and agricultural land. Because the value was essentially artificial, it was intended to be temporary. The first and only issue of *rentenmarks* had a value set at two billion, four hundred million dollars. The issue was divided equally between the government and the national banks to supply credit to industry. A currency commissioner was appointed with broad regulatory powers, and the government curtailed expenditures, cut salaries, and reduced employees by 300,000. To the surprise of many, especially the outside world, confidence was restored and inflation vanished with a gradual return of real market value for the mark. Also assisting economic development in the war torn countries was the US Dawes Plan of development loans with long terms and low interest rates (discussed in the previous chapter dealing with the United States). The noted American historian, William Carr, summarized Stresemann's achievements in this first part of his career. "Under Stresemann's guidance the republic had survived its darkest hour; threats to the unity of the *Reich* were overcome, confidence in the economy restored and reparations put on a realistic footing. These were considerable achievements, for which much, though by no means all, of the credit must go to Stresemann."

Locarno Treaties

With its economy recovering, the Weimar government was beginning to make friendly gestures toward France, and on October 16, 1925, in a small lakeside resort in Locarno, Switzerland, Germany signed peace and non-aggression treaties with its neighbors France, Belgium, Czechoslovakia, and Poland. Most of the populations of western Europe expressed great joy that at long last there was reason to believe that the principal warring parties, Germany and France, were prepared to live in peace with each other and to move toward rebuilding their respective economies. As the *New York Times* said, "France and Germany Bar War Forever." However, the single most important issue for the Germans was the complete withdrawal of all foreign troops from the Rhineland, which was ignored by the negotiators because France, although willing to consider withdrawal, was not ready to place a timeline on it. Stresemann, the former chancellor and now the German foreign minister and chief negotiator at Locarno, faced a response in Berlin that ranged from disappointment to outright hostility to the terms of the Locarno Treaty with France. The German people overwhelmingly believed that a de-militarized zone in the Rhineland, something Germany had accepted at Versailles, did not require occupation by foreign troops, mostly French. In a relatively short period of time, the Locarno Treaties, that had initially been so warmly received, fell into obsolescence with rapidly changing events.

Industrial Revival

By the end of the decade Germany was once again one of the world's great industrial nations. This remarkable revival was made possible by large investments of capital, much of it American, attracted by high interest rates and low labor costs. Heavy investments in basic industries, such as steel, coal, chemicals, and electrical products brought production levels in excess of pre-war figures. Merchant shipbuilding again became a major self-contained industry, with domestic raw materials being manufactured into complete modern ships that were in great demand everywhere. The rapid turn around was accomplished with some shortages of consumer products because the government rationed raw materials needed for basic industry. But up-to-date management techniques and more efficient methods brought about tremendous productivity that eventually found its way into products that raised the standard of living of most Germans.

An unanticipated effect of rapid industrial growth was a certain concentration or amalgamation of companies into empires of enterprises engaged in similar productive processes. I.G. Farben became the largest manufacturing concern in Europe with capital of over 900 million marks and products ranging from rayon to dynamite. Other industrial consolidations, approaching monopolies, resulted in economic power being controlled by an ever-diminishing number of hands. The prosperity of the German people became dependent upon the activities of a few gigantic cartels largely geared to export markets. Good for the national economy, not so good for the average German citizen.

The period of industrial development reached its zenith in 1930 when Germany, like all industrialized countries, felt the terrible impact of the Great Depression. President von Hindenburg, who had been elected in 1925, assumed dictatorial emergency powers at the outset of the depression, but his chancellor, Heinrich Bruning, adopted a policy of deflation that dried up the export market and led to a surge in unemployment. All of these rapid changes in the economy led to the ascent of the Nazi Party and Adolf Hitler in 1933. Still, the Weimar Republic had its share of important successes. It reformed the currency, unified tax policy, restored the railway system, and eliminated most of the requirements of the Treaty of Versailles. The decade also had more than its share of pleasures and unrestrained exuberance.

Culture and Society

Cultural activity can best be described as a continuance rather than a recovery because all aspects of artistic creation never really came to a halt during the war years, but continued to flourish, although perhaps at a slower rate. This was especially true in Berlin, which had been and remained, one of the most important cultural centers in Europe.

An entertainment feature that was created in Berlin during this time, and for which the City became famous all over Europe and America, was the sultry, saucy cabaret scene. The most famous of the many cabaret singers and dancers was Marlene Dietrich. Her stage presence exuded nonchalant hedonism that seemed to express the attitudes of a whole society. The cabaret genre and Dietrich herself were transported all over Europe and America, but the same lusty indifference could not be as effectively presented elsewhere as it was in Berlin.

Coexisting with popular night club entertainment was the ever present classical music for which Germans were justifiably proud – reminded always of the three B's; Bach, Beethoven, and Brahms. Concert performances that had never really stopped during the war were continued with gusto all over the country. Some of the great, young pianists in the world, like Rudolf Serkin, Claudio Arrau, and Vladimir Horowitz came to Berlin to study with, or just be near, the established virtuosos such as, Artur Schnabel. The same was true of promising conductors who sought out Bruno Walter and Otto Klemperer, and composers with modern and not always universally accepted styles. These included Stravinsky, Ravel, Bartok, and Prokofiev who were often seen in company with Arnold Schoenberg. Berlin was accepting of everything that was new, daring and different. The period could be compared to 19th century and pre-war Paris that opened its arms to young and unconventional painters and sculptors.

While there are many other cultural activities that could be mentioned, the period and the City made huge strides forward in the development of modern functional design in architecture. The leading figure here was Walter Gropius. His name will forever be linked with the somewhat vague term, "modern architecture" sometimes also called "Bauhaus," a German school of art and design that opened in the 1920s. It is characterized by function; simple, practical, but with stark creations of steel and glass that are bold and new. Most "skyscrapers" built in American cities and some European cities follow the useful functionality and graceful design that can trace its origin to Gropius and his many followers. Gropius described his ideas regarding residential design, but with equal applicability to large office structures, "The governing principle of the enterprise will be to make these houses comfortable, but not in terms of overdone gilded pomp but rather in clear and open spatial arrangements." These architectural concepts were beginning by the end of the decade to change the whole look of cities like Berlin and Weimar.

Societal changes in Germany in the 1920s were happening rapidly and were noticed by many citizens. Immigration and growing anti-Semitism would have profound impacts on later policies and directions taken by the fascist regime of the next decade and a half. One national group that flocked to Germany shortly after the war was the Russians. The Russian colony in Berlin in the twenties was quite large – numbering fifty thousand or more. Monarchists, anarchists, poets, businessmen, and former officers of the Czar's army sought temporary sanctuary from the upheavals back home. Dozens of Russian restaurants opened in Berlin along with small theaters and three daily Russian language newspapers. In these places, and on the open streets, one could usually find Russians in intense, and often heated, discussions about the failings of the past, and the extreme remedies for the future.

One of the most talented Russians to appear in Berlin was the nineteen-year old cellist Gregor Piatigorsky. He had crossed the German border by swimming a river while holding his cello over his head. Border guards fired their rifles into the water near him. He soon found help from the extraordinary network of refugee Russian musicians and his talent was quickly revealed. He is now honored as one of the greatest cellists of all time.

The Jewish population in Germany was not essentially immigrant but had lived and prospered there for many years. They tended to congregate in the large cities, especially Berlin. However, their numbers were never more than a small minority – less than one percent of the total. Approximately 173,000 Jews lived in Berlin and another 29,000 in Frankfort in 1925, but that was the zenith of Jewish population. During World War I, Jews volunteered in large numbers to fight in the German army. Their numbers far exceeded, proportionally, the general German population. Of the 100,000 Jews in the army, 80,000 served in front line trenches and 12,000 were killed – again a much higher casualty rate than that suffered by the Germans as a whole.

In spite of their small numbers, German Jews managed to acquire very visible positions of power and prestige. They dominated the giant banks; Deutsche, Dresdener, and Darmstadter, as well as many other commercial enterprises. In science, Jews were awarded one-quarter of all Nobel prizes won by Germans in the first twenty-five years of the century. Still, many Germans viewed the successes of their Jewish citizens as triumphs of an alien and vaguely threatening force.

Of course, the most famous Jewish scientist in Germany (Swiss by birth) was Albert Einstein. At the age of 26, Einstein was already famous in the scientific community because of his published *Theory of Relativity* in 1915. He was encouraged to come to Berlin by the great physicist, Max Planck, and offered his own laboratory at the Kaiser Wilhelm Institutes in the University of Berlin. He remained there in various positions until 1932 when the results of the elections convinced him to extend his teaching term at Cal Tech at the University of California, eventually ending at Princeton University. He was not always treated well in Germany however, when right-wing political groups saw Einstein as epitomizing all that was contemptible. He was a Jew, a liberal, an internationalist, a pacifist, an innovator and scientist whose work could not be understood by those of average intelligence. Nevertheless, he did not allow these ignorant slights to deter his activities. Although not a Zionist himself, he toured America raising funds with the Zionist leader Chaim Weizmann and later visited Palestine.

Even a brief look at the cultural and intellectual life of 1920s Germany, will certainly conclude that the devastation brought to the country by the Great War, did not destroy the energies, creativity, and joyful pursuits of German society as a whole.

Chapter 14. The Empire is Cracking

Governance

Great Britain and France thought of themselves as victors after World War I, and indeed they were better off than Germany, but it is fair to say that there were no real victors in Europe after that disastrous war. A Coalition government in Britain, headed by Liberal Prime Minister David Lloyd George, was heavily occupied in 1920 and '21 with responsibilities that the government accepted in the Versailles Treaty. These were many, but the principal ones included continued colonial control over India, Singapore, Hong Kong, and protection of the sea-lanes at Gibraltar and the Suez Canal. These were heavy responsibilities during normal times, but after the economic losses (Britain owed the US nearly $1,000,000,000.), and the great loss in population, especially males under 35, the foreign burdens were essentially unmanageable. Still, there was a strong sense of moral and political responsibility to honor commitments, particularly those negotiated by Lloyd George at Paris. Meanwhile the Dominions, Australia, New Zealand, South Africa, and Canada, were independent after the war, in all but their voluntary membership in the Commonwealth. However, most of the British government, led by the Coalition Cabinet, resisted any thought of change from its pre-war position of Empire, and firmly believed that all power and wealth would be restored with sufficient perseverance and effort.

But the overwhelming majority of the British public, including the citizens of the Dominions, were anxious for a return to normalcy. This did not include overseas "adventures" to right the wrongs in the world. The first real test of this foreign policy difference came when a group of Nationalists led by Mustafa Kemal, a Turkish hero at Gallipoli, resisted Greek attempts, supported politically by the British, to occupy most of western Turkey. The Turks rather quickly defeated the Greeks at Smyrna (Izmir) and moved to a position just south of Constantinople, where they waited for a British reaction.

After Kemal's victory over the Greeks and his movement north, the Cabinet took a clear decision to defend against the Turks. Their mandate under the Treaty to preserve the peace between the Greeks and the Turks, and to maintain what was left of the Ottoman Empire, were the principal arguments in support of military action against Kemal and the Turks. A call went out in September 1922 to the Dominions to contribute to the defense of Constantinople and the defeat of the insurgents. Canada, Australia, and New Zealand offered tepid verbal support to the British demand, but took no action to prepare an army. South Africa went even further by basically ignoring the British request. Once the Cabinet's position became public in England, voices in strong opposition were heard immediately. The *Times* printed a letter from the Conservative leader, Andrew Bonar Law, in which he argued, "We cannot act alone as the policeman of the world." The *Daily Mail* on September 18th said, "Not a single Dominion soldier should be allowed to lose his life in order that Mr. Churchill may make a new Gallipoli." The Coalition government that had been loosely stitched together since the war, began to fall apart over this issue and some others. The general election that followed did result in a victory for the Conservatives, but only after they had abandoned their bellicose approach to Turkey. The British citizenry, like all Europeans in the 1920s, were sick of war in any location and for any purpose other than pure self-defense.

During the latter years of the 1920s, there were no great strains in the Empire between the Dominions and the "mother" country. It appeared that a new, happy era had begun. This was aided in great part by the adoption of the "Balfour Definition" of 1926 that recognized the Dominions as "autonomous Communities within the British Empire." The age of British control over the four Dominions: South Africa, Australia, New Zealand, and Canada, (excluding India) was over, but economic influence from Britain remained strong for several decades.

Contemporaneous with the revolt of the Turkish Nationalists was the "Irish Problem." The struggle for the independence of Ireland from Great Britain did not begin in the 20th century but had been going on, unsuccessfully, for several centuries. There never was unanimity of opinion among the Irish about what "independence" really meant. Prior to World War I, there probably was a majority of Irish citizens who would have been satisfied, at least for several years, with Home Rule. This term was understood by most to mean obtaining a considerable level of local governmental autonomy, exercised by locally elected representatives, but with Ireland remaining fully included within the British Empire. The British Parliament would continue to have ultimate authority but would cede all local matters to an Irish Parliament. Efforts to achieve this change were successful in 1914 but with Britain becoming more absorbed with growing war concerns, lesser issues like Irish Home Rule, were put on the shelf to be implemented later.

Of course, there were also many Irish who believed that the meaning of independence was just that, complete separation from Britain and total autonomy of government in Ireland. Those who felt this way often referred back many years to American independence where important similarities could be drawn. The opponent, Britain, was the same; the objective was the same, total independence; and success was only achieved after a long and difficult war. There was also a split of opinion about the necessary means to achieve either of these objectives. The Home Rule advocates tended to believe in a non-violent political process, achieving success in a slower step-by-step approach. The independence fighters, generally referred to as the IRB (Irish Republican Brotherhood), believed that the British would never voluntarily give up any significant control over Ireland. Both sides had considerable evidence in past history to support their views.

In mid-1921, Lloyd George was determined to settle the Irish problem peacefully and consistent with the principle of self-determination that had guided so much of the discussion in Paris two years earlier. The British government offered the Irish leaders a cessation of violence and a conference in London to discuss a "free state," something more than Home Rule but less than full independence. The discussions lasted over two months but were never real negotiations. Lloyd George made clear that the British proposal was a "take it or leave it" proposition and if the Irish did not accept, the British would move many more troops into Ireland and force control. In essence, what was offered was a very broad Home Rule state which allowed an Irish Parliament to govern Ireland on virtually all matters except war, conscription, import-export protections, and loyalty to the crown. This latter point required an oath of loyalty to the King and was particularly troubling to many. However, the most controversial issue was the separation of six counties in Ulster that would remain an integral part of Great Britain. This was done because of the presumed preference of a majority of the citizens of those counties to remain fully united with Britain. A vote in Ulster later confirmed this presumption. The agreement, known as the Anglo-

Irish Treaty, was signed on December 6, 1921 but the reaction to it was almost equally divided among the Irish as to its acceptance.

Even though the Irish legislature (the Dail) and a vote of the people confirmed the acceptance of the Treaty, many were still opposed. Their primary opposition centered on the separation of Ulster from the rest of Ireland. A tragic civil war between the Irish, separating family members and friends on each side, ensued until May 24, 1923. The pro-treaty forces prevailed after much bloodshed. The Free State ultimately became the completely independent Republic of Ireland in 1937.

It was with India that Britain experienced the greatest difficulties as an imperial power. The war had stirred Indian nationalism and had brought together, if temporarily, the majority Hindu party and the Muslims who were inspired by the success of the Turks. Some efforts were made as early as 1919 to transfer certain powers to local ministers and elected Councils, but reserved to the Governor all authority over justice, police, and finance. The effect of these reforms, generous in British eyes but insignificant to the Indians, was to make clear to the native population that a long struggle would be necessary to achieve satisfactory sovereignty. With this backdrop the Hindu Congress launched a campaign for India's independence. Their unofficial leader was Mahatma Gandhi whose moral force was based upon non-violent resistance and economic boycotts of British goods. However, there was mob violence in February 1922 at a police station where 21 policemen were killed. Gandhi was able to stop the violence, but was nevertheless arrested and imprisoned for several months. During the remainder of the 1920s there was less violence, but an increasing determination to achieve independence politically and non-violently. This goal was finally achieved in 1947.

As with the US, Britain experienced a growing concern about the spread of communist ideology from the Soviet Union. Some called this "Russophobia" and tended to dismiss it as a serious threat to capitalism in Britain. Others however, saw in every example of labor unrest a potential connection to the stated orthodoxy of Marx; that economic revolutions would be spread by the world's workers, particularly in developed capitalist countries. This latter opinion was given much greater credence when on May 4, 1926 a general strike was declared throughout Britain. It was initially a wage strike by the nation's coal miners, but turned very serious and occasionally violent after railroad workers, transport workers, iron and steel workers, builders, and printers, numbering over 2,500,000, refused to work in support of the miners. Some union leaders expected the government to collapse, but after only eight days the general strike was called off. The miners continued their strike for six months but finally returned having gained nothing in wage concessions. The country as a whole, while sympathizing with the miners, would not tolerate rebellion on the part of trade unions as a class. Most understood that the strike was very much local, raising entirely domestic issues dealing with the miner's working conditions and wages. It did not involve the larger matters of basic economic policy. Nevertheless, no existing inequalities in management-labor relations were resolved, and seeds were planted among many intellectuals who favored socialist policies that they believed would address the huge gap in the distribution of wealth.

The governance of the Empire, such as it was, was also somewhat unstable with the Parliament changing majority parties and Prime Ministers frequently. Control of the government shifted from Liberal to Conservative to Labour, and then back to Conservative in October of 1924. The Tories held that position until 1929 when the Labour Party again was elected. It was also during this time that Winston Churchill was defeated as a Liberal in 1922, but then was elected as a Conservative in 1924. Churchill's reemergence was complete when the Prime Minster, Stanley Baldwin, named him Chancellor of the Exchequer (essentially budget minister).

The Economy and Industry

The British economy was already beginning to show signs of a slump by 1922. The value of its exports, always a key barometer, declined 44 percent from the immediate years after the war, and wages also declined about an equal amount. Unemployment, which had never been a serious problem in Britain since the industrial revolution of the 19th century, suddenly was quite serious. The unemployment rate hovered around 16 percent for most of the year. Industries hit particularly hard were shipbuilding, iron and steel production, and engineering. Railroad expansion, which should have been at its peak at this time because of acute transportation needs, was practically non-existent, except for several new lines for London's underground system. Likewise, the commercial airline industry, which was beginning a rapid growth in the US, was moribund in Britain. This was not due to a lack of technical knowledge, but rather, less need to service a smaller land-mass, other than by rail.

Chancellor of the Exchequer Churchill, produced his first budget in April 1925. It incorporated several bold new policies, including a reduction in the income tax, a new contributory pension scheme, significant reductions for the military, especially the Admiralty, and, most important, a return to the gold standard. This austerity budget was supported by most economists at the time, with the notable exception of John Maynard Keynes who opposed reduced government spending on the eve of a recession (a dispute still raging today). Also noted by his opponents, Churchill, who always supported the agency that he headed, had been the most vocal proponent of huge expenditures for the navy when he led the Admiralty. Now that he directed the Treasury, he was promoting naval reductions.

The return to the gold standard is viewed today by most experts as a huge mistake. It had the immediate effect of overvaluing the pound by ten percent and raising the cost of the country's exports. Whereas, Britain had enjoyed financial supremacy in the years before the war, being a creditor nation with a large trade surplus, these conditions no longer applied. New York and other cities had become rivals and creditors, with London dependent on short-term loans to keep its economy moving.

The views of organized labor were bitter, especially when cutbacks in social services were announced, "...whilst the rich betake themselves to St. Moritz and the ladies of Mayfair spend extravagantly on dresses...they make the children pay by cuts in education." (*Economist*, February 18, 1922).

Gradually, it became clear that Britain had been in a state of economic decline ever since the beginning of the century. For many years, there had been an increasing dependence on foreign trade, exchanging manufactured products and coal for foodstuffs and raw materials. But the war increased global competitiveness and spurred many countries to self-sufficiency. Britain's advantages in the years of the industrial revolution were over and coal was less in demand because oil had become the primary source used in virtually all new industries. It was very difficult for many leaders in business and government to accept the new reality that Great Britain was no longer at the economic pinnacle of the world. This postwar mood is powerfully described in *This Age of Conflict*, by the noted English writers, Frank Chambers, Christina Phelps Harris, and Charles Bayley: "Blinded by tradition and prestige, they strained themselves even further in efforts to resume their former accustomed ways and habits. ...Again and again after 1919, seemingly out of sheer inflexibility and false pride, Britain intensified her weariness, delayed and misdirected her possible recovery."

The Military

Lloyd George most probably expressed the views of the vast majority of Britons in 1919 when he told the heads of the armed services to plan on the assumption that there would be no war within the next ten years. This became known as the "Ten Year Rule." The cash-strapped political leaders were only too willing to cut back military expenditures significantly. The only serious potential threat on the horizon concerned Japan, which could, and probably would, begin to dominate in the Far East. In the mid-twenties Britain had no naval base for capital ships east of Malta, so would have had a difficult task of countering Japanese aggression in the area. The Admiralty pressed to establish such a base at Singapore, but they were rebuffed by the Cabinet. Churchill wrote in December 1924: "A war with Japan! But why should there be a war with Japan? I do not believe there is the slightest chance of it in our lifetime." (Churchill was not always correct in his predictions.) The base was later approved and construction began in 1933.

The naval service had always, historically and traditionally, been the most important branch of the overall military services. In the 1920s, Britain still had more capital warships than any other country, but most of these ships were nearing obsolescence. Also, after the war, a separate Flying Corps was created under command of the Army. This had the effect of diverting most defense funds for aircraft from the Navy to the Army. Consequently, there were fewer planes available for aircraft carriers, and, therefore, less reason to build very many carriers. It is not so much that the Admiralty was unconvinced of the value of carriers and naval aircraft, as some have assumed, but rather that the Army made a more convincing case for "strategic bombing" by land based aircraft against land targets. Whatever the reasons, the result was that by the mid 1930s, Britain had fallen far behind the US and Japan in aircraft carrier development and construction. The Admiralty tried to narrow this gap by quickly building smaller carriers with fewer and smaller aircraft, but their effectiveness was limited to reconnaissance and anti-submarine warfare. They were simply no match at sea against larger and better protected carriers with far more aircraft.

This naval weakness became a major handicap in the next war, particularly in the Pacific theater where Britain was forced to rely almost entirely on the US Navy.

Society and Culture

By mid-decade the war had receded into the background and the changes that it brought had been accepted. It was taken for granted, for instance, that the old order of high society of the Edwardian days had gone forever. Large estates were being broken up, large houses sold or converted in the country into schools and nursing homes. Even tax policy, such as higher income taxes and death taxes, were causing a significant redistribution of property. Farmland that had been bought by tenants, who had mortgaged their future in the pre-war years, was now available to sell at 40-50 percent higher then the initial cost. This was so, primarily, because there were now far more potential buyers in the market.

In the field of British elementary and secondary public education, growth and opportunities for increased numbers of students was often measured in the availability of "free places." There was always quality education for those who could afford it, but in the early 1920s several reports on the state of public education in Britain showed that economic growth was severely retarded as the percentage of the educated young declined or remained stagnant. Consequently, the number of free places began to increase significantly: 131,309 free places (37%) in 1922 and 178,204 free places (43%) in 1930. The direct result of the increases in student numbers at the secondary level was, of course, greater increases at the college and university levels. Many academic changes along more practical course offerings were also adopted, and the overall impact was a profound change in the British workforce to more professional and technically skilled employees.

The culture of the British Isles had been, for centuries, at the highest level in the western world, and this certainly continued in the 1920s, but with directional changes. This point can best be illustrated by considering two major art forms: literature and drama. Among British literary figures of the time, two best displayed fresh and controversial styles, and each, in his own way, established a pattern of stylistic approaches seldom seen before. These two were James Joyce (born in Ireland but spent most of his life in London) and D. H. Lawrence. Joyce's best-known works are; *Dubliners, Portrait of the Artist as a Young Man, Finnegans Wake*, and his greatest novel, the classic, *Ulysses*. In all of Joyce's novels, the societal pictures that are drawn are carefully crafted through the language of his principal characters. Especially in *Ulysses*, there are mock-heroic accounts of low activities described in high language, and accounts of high ideals described in low language. The hypocrisy is hard to miss. Joyce's purpose was certainly to appeal to the desire in all of us to see the nobility taken down a peg or two.

D. H. Lawrence, another giant of the period, was a poetic novelist as well as a distinguished poet. Like Joyce, his word craft was fresh and innovative, but in the realm of Protestant tradition as opposed to Joyce's Catholic tradition. Lawrence's best novels are, most would agree, *Aaron's Rod, Kangaroo*, and his classic, *Lady Chatterley's Lover*. A common theme is the final decay, as Lawrence sees it, in the post-war years of the old Christian and liberal-humanist ideals. Words like love, liberty, justice, and brotherhood have lost their true meaning in a cynical and self-centered world. Another frequent theme for Lawrence is the loss of masculine independence, by which he means, not giving in to society, political movements, and above all to women.

Clearly, the one thing James Joyce and D. H. Lawrence had in common was the initial reaction of a majority of the English public to their most famous books. They were considered salacious and pornographic. Ulysses and Lady Chatterley's Lover were both banned for a time in many countries, including Britain and the United States. The bannings did not last long, and as always happens, tended to increase interest and sales.

The field of British drama in the early part of the 20th century is, indeed, crowded with well-known writers, but two very different playwrights offer a chance to see the parameters of skills provided to the play-loving public. The titan of the time was certainly George Bernard Shaw. Another of a new genre, was Sean O'Casey. (Both were born in Ireland but resided in England most of their lives.) Shaw was a most prolific playwright, he produced over 80 plays, but a few of his best are *Arms and the Man*, *Heartbreak House*, *Man and Superman*, and *Back to Methuselah*. His audiences enjoyed the subtle humor injected into often ponderous discourse. In *Methuselah*, Shaw develops his theme of a benign "Life Force" which directs the evolution of man by trial and error. This massive five-play work begins in the Garden of Eden and ends thousands of years in the future. Shaw and a few others revolutionized British drama by changing what had been sentimental entertainment into a forum for considering moral, political, and economic issues.

By contrast it is useful to consider another playwright, Sean O'Casey, who wrote far fewer plays, but is also considered by many to be a major contributor to modern drama. His best known plays are: *The Shadow of a Gunman*, *Juno and the Paycock*, and *The Plough and the Stars*, all produced between 1923 and 1926. They feature unconventional and highly critical reactions to the Irish Easter Rising and the later civil war. The negative response of the ordinary people is based on their very real fear of economic troubles and their personal detachment from the concept of political independence.

The 1920s for Britain was a time of dramatic changes across society from decline in world economic supremacy to a growing self-criticism of long held values. This period was the threshold to the next decade of depression, giving impetus to challenges from the left to change the bedrock of capitalism to a more egalitarian system.

Chapter 15. Secular Turkey in the Muslim World

Turkish Independence

Aplausible argument can be made that, of the seven countries discussed here, Turkey experienced the most profound change in the 1920s. To appreciate this, it is necessary to look to governance and other relevant factors that made up the Ottoman Empire prior to World War I. By the turn of the 20th century, the Sultan's rule (Sultan Abdulhamid) had degenerated into an oriental despotism that raised western doubts about the viability of the Ottoman Empire. Parts of the Empire in North Africa, such as Tunisia and Egypt, had already been lost to France and Britain respectively. Internally the Sultan's authority, both politically and religiously, was being challenged by opponents like the "Young Turks" who had many followers among officers of the army. The Young Turks believed that significant rejuvenation of the country had to be based on Turkish nationalism and not on Islam. This was not a rejection of Islam but rather, a separation of governmental and religious authority.

Before the war, the country was economically depleted and militarily disorganized. Leadership was greatly lacking so the Sultan and his ministers looked to the one European power that had shown support in the past – Germany. The Germans saw great value in Turkey as an ally because the Turks controlled the route from the Mediterranean to the Black Sea, thereby cutting off a major supply route to Russia. Also German warships could escape through the Dardanelles if attacked by the more powerful British navy. Another event forced the hand of the Turks to side with Germany. In July of 1914, just days before the start of the War, the British took control of two warships being built under contract to Turkey. The Germans immediately offered two of their own ships that were in the Black Sea for use by the Turks. Those ships and their German crews shelled Russian ports on the Black Sea several times in the name of Turkey. Shortly thereafter Russia, France, and Britain all declared war on Turkey.

Because the War ended badly for Germany and its ally Turkey, the terms of peace for Turkey in the Treaty of Versailles were also unacceptable to most Turks, especially the Nationalists. The Treaty stipulated that Greece was to receive the major portion of European Turkey and that Constantinople would be under a British mandate of military control. France and Italy were to carve out "spheres of economic influence" from the Anatolian provinces. Turkish outrage had a unifying effect on hitherto disparate groups and all that was needed was a leader who could bring organization and purpose to a nationalist cause. Mustafa Kemal, the Colonel now General, hero of Gallipoli, seized the moment and began organizing an army in Anatolia. The Ottoman government, still loyal to, or at least dependent on, Britain charged Kemal with treason and sentenced him *in absentia* to death. But it was the death of the Ottoman government that was soon to be. The history of the fight for Turkish independence was discussed in Chapter 3.

With the signing of the Lausanne Peace Treaty on July 24, 1923 between Turkey, Britain, France, Greece, Italy, and many smaller countries around the Aegean Sea, most of the decisions made in Paris in 1919 dealing with the Ottoman Empire were undone, and the new independent Turkish Nation was recognized by all the world powers. The boundaries of modern Turkey were also recognized by the Treaty and the Aegean was declared an open sea to all shipping.

Governance

The primary institutional obstacle to creating a Republic in Turkey was the six-centuries old sultanate. Mustafa Kemal was nominally Muslim, but by the fall of 1922 he saw the Sultan as the embodiment of the backwardness of his country and a puppet to the western powers. This view of the sultanate was shared by most Turks but not understood by British and French political leaders. Those leaders made a huge mistake when they invited the Sultan to attend the Lausanne Conference without the consent of the National Assembly. Kemal acted quickly to seize the anger generated by this serious slight. He proposed to the Assembly the abolition of the sultanate and the expulsion of the last Sultan. The Assembly appointed a Commission to study the matter but Kemal threatened its members with arrest if they did not comply immediately. They did so and the Sultan was gone before the Peace Conference got underway.

However, the institution of the caliphate was not as easy to resolve as the sultanate. The Caliph was the generally recognized religious leader and primary interpreter of Islamic law. For centuries the positions of Sultan and Caliph had been combined. With the Sultan now gone, the successor Caliph was making moves to require actions of the National Assembly to conform to Islamic law, as interpreted by the Caliph. This authority was supported by Islamic clergy, mostly Arab, from outside of Turkey. Kemal and his subordinates argued vigorously that the Assembly was responsible only to the nation and that the law of the revolution was above all other laws. Inherent also in their arguments was the fact that those outside of Turkey had no standing to impose their views on the Turkish people. After much debate, which Kemal left to his supporters, the National Assembly voted on March 3, 1924 to depose the Caliph and abolish the caliphate from Turkey.

This posed a potential problem, the creation of a vacuum in the religious center of society. The problem was dealt with by Kemal, when he authorized the establishment of the Directorate of Religious Affairs on the very day that the caliphate was abolished. The Directorate was under his control, but had been given free rein to permit differing interpretations of Islamic law. Thus, the influence of religion, long a rigid and uncompromising factor in Islamic societies, was sidelined from government and made an academic and intellectual pursuit. Mustafa Kemal's control over all elements of Turkey's government was absolute by 1925. As President of the National Assembly and head of the only political party authorized by law, he was virtually a dictator and free to move his country in any direction he wished.

While it is probably true, as many have asserted, the supreme leader intended to lead his country to a real democracy, he was uncertain that his countrymen were ready so soon after the fall of the Empire. Consequently, he practiced a kind of "benevolent autocracy" as opposed to a true dictatorship. He also distrusted Communism and Fascism-Nazism and kept those ideologies at arms length to save his country from their contagions.

In the arena of foreign policy, Kemal's advisors urged him to form alliances with one or more of the great powers. However, the president, perhaps remembering the disastrous alliance with Germany during the War, chose friendly relations with all of Turkey's neighbors and assumed a neutralist attitude toward all other nations. The one exception to this policy was Greece where mutual distrust, and sometimes outright hostility, existed for many years.

Reform and Westernization

From Kemal's earliest years as an Army officer, he was convinced that forward progress, whether economically, militarily, or governmentally, required the complete shedding of the old ways and an acceptance of modern, western practices and policies. This meant the implementation of scientific approaches to industrialization, economics, and a completely new constitution based on western legal principles and devoid of the restraints of Islamic law. Without the all-powerful governmental authority that he had insisted upon, changes to this extent might have been impossible, but certainly would have required many years to accomplish. Nevertheless, between the years 1928 and 1938, Turkey changed into a European-like state and, very importantly, a secular country with complete separation of government and religion.

Symbols of the past, such as the fez and other non-western clothing, were abolished. Arabic was abandoned and the use of Roman letters was mandatory. Complete equality of women with men was granted and, in 1934, women received the right to vote and hold office at the highest levels. Sunday was declared the day of rest, not the Mohammedan Friday. In 1928 Turkey became the first country with an overwhelming Muslim population to declare in the Constitution that religion was a private matter and Islam was not the official religion of the state. Kemal even ventured into the arena of Turkish art. The Mullahs had forbidden the portrayal of living objects in any art form, so Kemal had many statues of himself created and placed in prominent locations in towns all over the country. Many of these statues remain today. Western music was also introduced, however the hearts of the people did not change overnight and Kemal lost interest in these reforms.

Perhaps the greatest changes that were implemented immediately were those in the field of education. Primary school became free and required for both boys and girls. The Koran was forbidden to be taught in public schools but mathematics and science courses were required. Languages had always been taught, but now western languages were also offered. Higher education changed dramatically as well, but not so much by government decree as from the demands of the secular intelligentsia. Universities had been heavily influenced by the Imans, many of whom were poorly educated. Turkish scholars had resisted their influence for years and were now in a position to remove them, which they did.

Another important change, both symbolic and substantive, was the establishment of the National Capital at Ankara, and not at Istanbul. The reasons for this move, although not publically explained, were essentially that Istanbul was easily occupied by foreign powers during the War and could be again, and foreign commercial interests had dominated the city for centuries under the sultans. Kemal was determined to show that Turks would now be in charge of all aspects of Turkey's interests, both governmental and economic. This meant, not just Turks but Turks loyal to the new regime. This was not always the case in post Ottoman Istanbul.

Industry and the Economy

The Ottoman Turk did not engage in menial occupations or trade. He was the soldier or administrator; the peasant tilled the soil and did the manual labor. Thus, only foreigners or Christians carried on the economy of the Empire. This economy consisted of exporting agricultural products, carpets, handicrafts, and some minerals. Finished goods were imported from many other countries. Kemal and his associates set out almost immediately to change this so that all citizens regardless of race or creed could partake in a building economy. They realized that even tied to a major world power, such as Germany, disastrous shortages and economic collapse could occur.

So the Government did everything possible at first to encourage the growth of private industry. (The exact opposite of what was happening with their neighbor, the USSR.) Protective tariffs were imposed, grants of land were made for industry, transportation rates were reduced, and within a decade, a small but growing private industrial sector was thriving. However, the development of modern financial institutions, even by the standards of the 1920s, was slow to emerge. The Government had very little funding available, virtually no international credit, and private capital was rarely used for equity investments. Those with excess funds were either reinvesting in additional land or hoarding money as gold in home safes. More reasons, as Kemal saw it, to increase the speed of westernization and education.

Land ownership, the basis for many years of secure prosperity, presented a mixed picture. Turkish laws had for decades permitted and encouraged ownership by those who lived on the land and produced its goods. But intensive subdivision to allow descendants to own their parcels resulted in millions of acres of cultivable land being divided into parcels with an average size of 16 acres. This was highly inefficient with most farmers producing only a little more than they required for their own family's needs. Efforts were made over a number of years to force consolidation of agrarian lands and to increase more efficient farming methods.

Trade unions had been illegal under the Ottomans and the Government of the Republic made no effort to revive them. There was a reasonable fear that the Communists in the Soviet Union would attempt to take over the unions, as they had done in other countries but with only small successes. Nevertheless, the threat was real and close by. The Government took steps over several years to establish state labor regulations covering such matters as hours of work, public holidays, employment of women and children, health and safety, and a system of arbitration of conditions of employment. These labor laws of the 1920s and 30s were well ahead of most industrial countries including the US.

The proposition advanced at the beginning of this section, that the changes which occurred in Turkey in the 1920s surpassed all other countries considered here, is a powerful case when one considers the feudal and decrepit Ottoman Empire at the beginning of the decade, compared to the modern and rapidly improving Turkey in the early 1930s.

Chapter 16. The French Empire at Its Zenith

Democratic Government in a Very Uncertain Time

The French and their President Georges Clemenceau were said to be reasonably satisfied with the Treaty of Versailles as it was written, but the disillusionment did not take long to set in. The two most important objectives for the French from the discussions in Paris were: security from their aggressive neighbor to the east, Germany, and the collection of the promised reparations so necessary for the reconstruction of their war torn country. Ultimately, neither of these objectives were to be satisfied. However in the 1920s, France experienced an impressive recovery; with the modernization of many industries, improvement in agricultural production beyond prewar levels, harnessing of water power for electrical plants, and a great revival of the tourist industry. The election of 1922 brought to power a rightist party that formed a government and was known as the Bloc National. The new President was Alexandre Millerand, a staunch conservative. The Bloc's power base came from industrialists, bankers, the Catholic Church, and some labor unions. Millerand addressed the pressing economic problems by continuing the wartime program of borrowing money, creating a special German budget to receive the reparation payments, and paying down the debt. When Germany reduced its payments to a small fraction of the agreed upon amount, Millerand named a Premier with substantial financial expertise, Raymond Poincaré. His first act was to try to force German payments by occupation of the Ruhr, the primary industrial region of Germany. But this was a failure because most of the heavy industry was shut down and could not be started by either country without a massive infusion of money that neither had.

In 1924 the Millerand government fell to be replaced briefly by a socialist government that faired even worse after increasing taxes and watching the value of the frank decline precipitously. Poincaré was returned by the Chamber of Deputies and given decree powers over financial matters. Finally, economic conditions turned around when Poincaré placed a curb on borrowing, cut civil and military budgets, and established a sinking fund to retire the massive debt. The end of the decade, 1926 – 1929, was the happiest and most stable postwar period for France. Unfortunately, that all changed for France and most of the western world with the arrival of the great depression.

In the matter of military security, France would again be disappointed. Clemenceau had pressed hard for a French occupation of the Rhineland to help secure its eastern border from future German aggression. Lloyd George and Wilson rejected this on the grounds that the armistice had been based on the agreement that all combatants would return to their prewar borders. The Rhineland was clearly part of Germany. Having failed to convince the other leaders, Clemenceau was forced to agree to a demilitarized zone in the Rhineland and written assurances from Britain and the US to defend this territory from any future German attack. In addition, the terms of the Treaty and all subsidiary agreements were to be monitored and enforced by the proposed League of Nations. No League enforcement measure was ever seriously considered. But the US failed to ratify this side agreement and, of course, refused to participate as a member of the League of Nations. Britain also seemed to be reverting to its old policy of a balance of powers and was encouraging rapid German economic recovery. This was indeed true, however it was not an anti-French policy but rather a concern about Soviet expansionism.

Since its former military allies seemed to have diverted attention elsewhere, the French military decided to prepare it's own defenses against what many military leaders believed was the almost inevitable second attack. Andre Maginot was the Minister of War in 1929 and was assigned the unenviable task of developing a major defensive line running from Belgium in the north to an area south of Alsace. The so-called Maginot Line was never fully completed and was never intended to be an impregnable wall against a ground attack. But the French people were led to believe that it was the new "Wall of France." In the decade of construction, French citizens could observe huge concrete structures, gun-turrets, tank traps, and all the latest defensive warfare equipment being installed, especially in the Alsace-Lorraine region. The cost was over $500 million dollars. There was one early and vocal critic of the effort, a young colonel, Charles de Gaulle. He correctly predicted the tactics used later to bring mechanized vehicles in a rapid attack at various weak points, and then create an encirclement behind the defenses.

So the French public was confidently given to believe that modern military science had at last discovered a means to deter, or at least substantially delay, any new attacks from their German adversary who had attacked more than thirty times in the last century. These errors of military and political planning were largely responsible for the tragedy that followed in 1940.

Colonialism after the War

During the fifteen to twenty year period between the end of the First World War and the beginning of the Second, the French Empire reached its greatest geographical expansion. Its colonial empire comprised over 12,540,000 sq. km, nine percent of the earth's land mass. While this physical size was indeed impressive, most French officials understood that the colonies as a whole were a serious economic drain on French resources. There were also varying degrees of local movements toward independence. It was clear to objective observers that France's imperial trajectory was headed downward.

A listing of the Colonies and Protectorates by region includes:

North Africa
Algeria, Morocco, and Tunisia

French West Africa
Mauritania, Sudan, Niger, Senegal, French Guinea, and Ivory Coast

French Equatorial Africa
Chad, Gabon, and Cameroon

Middle East
Syria and Lebanon

French Indochina
Cambodia, Laos, and Viet Nam.

The motives of the French Government in the 1920s is concerned to a great extent with the struggle to retain and improve the connection between the mother country and each of its colonies. There were two major, conflicting points of view about how best to achieve this. One view expressed the belief that assimilation of indigenous peoples into French culture, language, education, and even, over time, religious practices, was the best long- term approach to success. The other point of view is usually called "associationism." It is described as a colonial administration that sought to cultivate an indigenous elite, provide security, contain potential opposition, and create the strongest economic benefits possible for the mother country. Obviously, the latter approach could be achieved in a shorter time frame, but retained the elements of coercion. Those supporting the associationist policy emphasized that compromises with local elites were necessary to make governance and economic expansion work.

The consideration here will focus on, arguably, the two most important colonies to France; Algeria and Syria. While colonial administration varied from region to region, the goals of associationism were consistently applied, especially regarding the largest and potentially valuable colonies. The first significant occupation of Syria by the French came in October 1918, in anticipation, no doubt, of the cessation of hostilities one month later. This incursion was meant to solidify French claims of a mandate over Syria, and also meant to head off Emir Faisal who was trying to consolidate the Arab portions of the Ottoman Empire. The occupation also included Lebanon and was accomplished without resistance. At the time, Lebanon was a majority Christian country while Syria was overwhelmingly Muslim. Understandings were secretly reached later with Turkey and Mustafa Kemal not to assist the Arab/Muslims in controlling Syria. In exchange, Kemal covertly received arms and other assistance in his war with Greece and confrontation with Britain. (So much for the unity of the Big Three only a short time after Versailles.) The Syrian mandate was governed for the rest of the decade through problematic but self-serving partnerships. Control was exercised through a well-educated political community and wealthy, leading families, largely to the exclusion of the Muslim/Arab majority.

The experience in Algeria was very different, not just from Syria but from all other French colonies. A major reason for this was the long-term relationship between the countries – Algeria had become a French colony in 1830. Significant assimilation to French culture, language, and financial structure had occurred over the last 100 years. A popular comment was often used to describe this relationship; "Just as the Seine divides Paris, so the Mediterranean divides France and Algeria, two parts of the same whole." Still there was a serious and growing trend developing that would, ultimately, cause a rupture. That trend consisted of large numbers of immigrants to Algeria; many, but not all, were

French settlers who found excellent opportunities not far from home. However, complete Algerian independence did not occur until April of 1962, after many bloody skirmishes that included French settlers who did not want independence and French troops who were carrying out their government's policy granting full independence.

The policy of French colonial troops fighting for France in the World War became problematic in several ways. The African colonies supplied far more soldiers to the cause than Middle Eastern or Asian colonies, and they consistently fought bravely and loyally. In fact, North African and West African soldiers suffered greater losses per capita than those from France, and French losses were also huge. The problems arouse immediately after the armistice because promises of large cash rewards and land availability had been made by colonial managers to meet recruitment goals during the War. But France was nearly bankrupt in 1919, and the best land in the colonies was still owned by wealthy individuals and large organizations who were determined to keep their assets. Although the French economy improved fairly quickly, the immediate post-war period was fraught with fears of riots and local rebellions.

The problems of compensation were eventually worked out, but a more serious concern involved expectations on both sides. French hopes were that ex-servicemen would form a distinct cadre of military and police officials who were culturally assimilated and reconciled to colonial order. But the soldier's experience of discriminatory treatment, dreadful conditions, and delayed demobilization clashed with colonial management expectations. The short sighted policy of the French Colonial Management Ministry was to push the native troops out of France and back to their homes in virtually the same depressed environment that they had left. This engendered long-term anger and distrust that led all French colonies eventually to revolt and to seek independence in their own time.

French Culture

After the War, France and especially Paris, enjoyed a cultural revival almost immediately due to pent up desires for personal expression and rejection of traditional mores. Some of these expressions, particularly in new literature, took the form of what Gertrude Stein called, "the Lost Generation." This referred to the alienation of young men and women who had lived through and sometimes witnessed firsthand the human devastations that resulted from the most horrendous war in history. Expatriate activity also reached new highs because many foreigners saw Paris as the center of new ideas that could be expressed in art, music, and, of course, literature. Many came for brief stays but most chose Paris as a new home, at least for several years. Among the best known foreign writers who came at this time were; Fyodor Dostoyevsky, John Dos Passos, F. Scott Fitzgerald, Ernest Hemingway, William Faulkner, James Joyce, Oscar Wilde, Samuel Beckett, Franz Kafka, Henry Miller, and many more. France was also more permissive regarding censorship and many foreign language novels were originally published in France while being banned in America and Britain.

The rejuvenated world of art continued and expanded the surrealist movement popularized by Pablo Picasso and others, portraying the unconscious mind as manifested in dreams and characterized by an irrational, fantastic arrangement of material. This movement became known as the School of Paris and was manifested as a clear attack on bourgeois cultural values. The International Exposition of Decorative Arts held in Paris in 1925 helped to shape and popularize a distinctive decorative style that came to be known as Art Deco. Many buildings and interior spaces are still admired for these unique architectural approaches. Parisians of all classes were justly proud of their leadership in cultural pursuits and this pride, as much as any other single thing, helped to restore the joys of living that had been greatly restrained just a few years earlier.

France moved politically in the first half of the decade in a very uncertain, even contradictory, way from the extreme right to the left and back again to a more moderate rightist government. Leadership was lacking at first but the second half of the decade saw substantial improvement across the economy and the security of the Nation. It is accurate to say that France, the most physically damaged country, had recovered by 1930 far better and quicker than most had originally predicted. Consequently, when the worldwide depression hit in the early 1930s, France was able to absorb the financial and commercial losses better than many other countries.

Chapter 17. Italy Embraces Fascism

Although Italy had been a member of the Triple Alliance with Germany and Austria-Hungary formed by Otto von Bismarck in 1882, it had always been viewed at home and by the other countries as a weak and uncertain partner. By 1914 when war broke out, Italy had experienced numerous disputes with Austria over territorial and commercial matters and was deeply divided about entering into a war, and if so, on which side. The extreme conservatives and extreme liberals agreed on this one issue that Italy should avoid any connection to the hostilities. Nevertheless, the pro-war element prevailed and in May of 1915 war was declared against Austria-Hungary. The political leadership naively believed that Italy's participation could be limited to Austria-Hungary. Later, in August of 1916, Italy declared war on Germany, in part to be in a better position after the war regarding territorial changes.

Italy's combat operations were primarily in the mountainous areas at their border with Austria. These operations, like most of the movements in other combat zones, were inconclusive. Internal political differences about the war continued, even to the point of serious accusations against the Vatican as being in sympathy with Austria. There was no significant proof of this. Consequently, when the war ended, Italy was on the winning side and had a seat at the Peace Conference in Paris. However, it was understood by the Big Three, if never expressed, that Italy had played a minor role in the fighting and ultimate result.

At the end of the war, the Italian army was in disarray having suffered an unprecedented number of desertions. One estimate had it that over 500,000 men were in hiding, especially in southern Italy and Sicily. Italian industry was no better off. In the absence of strong leadership, factory workers were demanding a share in management and adoption of socialist principles. Strikes lead to riots, looting, and bloodshed. With this background the Italian Government gave up its interests in Albania, and the Kingdoms of the Serbs, Croats, and Slovens by signing the Treaty of Rapallo in November of 1920. The Kingdoms later became Yugoslavia. The affairs of Italy, in the eyes of most Italians, could hardly have sunk lower.

Governance

By 1922 Benito Mussolini had achieved leadership status in the *fascisti*, as the fascists were called, in the northern Italy/Milan region. In September, he boldly made demands of the government, which included dissolution of the Chamber of Deputies and early elections. His speech in Milan ended with the dramatic, "On to Rome." When his demands were refused, the fascists organized quickly into a unified force, something that had not existed before, and ordered a march. They stated that the march was not made against the army, nor the police, nor the King, nor against the "productive bourgeoisie," nor against the workers in the fields and offices. It was clear that the only real target was the government, already very unpopular. Mussolini did not join the march but when he was called on October 29th and asked to accept a ministry, he immediately took the train to Rome with the parting remark, "Tomorrow Italy will not have a ministry but a government."

The next day a new, powerful ministry was created and Mussolini was appointed Chief of Staff, effectively prime minister. He immediately ordered the removal of 50,000 *fascisti* from Rome in order to establish his political dominance without the need of force. On November 23, 1922 the King and Chamber granted Mussolini dictatorial powers for one year (the year never ended). As previously discussed, Mussolini reached accommodations with both the Vatican and the independent press that guaranteed their silence and *de facto* acceptance of his actions. Italy's revolution was over and the dictatorship of Benito Mussolini had begun.

The Economy

The Italian Fascists firmly believed that Italy's immediate industrialization and economic modernization only required the creation of an investment climate, restoration of political stability, and provision of a disciplined labor force to bring about rapid growth in the economy. Because their goal was not universal equality and human liberation as preached but not practiced by the Bolsheviks, they were harshly critical of socialist and communist principles.

Major businesses were organized into syndicates, also called associations, which were grouped by industry. Mussolini authorized thirteen confederations of employers, employees, and professional workers who were authorized to bargain collectively, but were prohibited by law to strike or to engage in lockouts. This organizational structure, combined with government control of labor unions, gave the government a strong influence over the kind and quantity of production. Labor unrest through strikes and lockouts were to be resisted at all costs because that greatly reduced production and gave the workers a potential platform for political opposition. Also the Corporate State allowed the government to direct much of the nation's economic life without a formal change of ownership.

Shortly after coming to power, Mussolini appointed Alberto De Stefani as his Minister of Finance. De Stefani was a professor and well regarded economist who was known to support free trade principles. However, after assuming his office both he and Mussolini were careful to present the new government as fiscally orthodox, determined to cut wasteful spending, willing to denationalize the telephone network, and cancel investigations into excessive war profits. Rather than opening up new markets to private enterprise in a free economy, De Stefani now preached tight governmental controls and a passion to balance the budget.

The Corporate State was a progressive (for the time) high sounding compromise which gave the state wide powers over the economy, yet respected vested interests up to a point. Mussolini described it falsely as a benevolent, classless economic system that contrasted well against western, democratic capitalism. He regarded it as Fascism's greatest contribution to political science. Indeed the Corporate State did produce a balanced state budget by 1925, a rate of savings and capital accumulation that was unsurpassed in Italy until the 1950s, and a rate of industrial growth that doubled from mid-decade to 1929. This industrial growth exceeded the rate of growth for all other European countries during the same time period.

The Concordat with the Vatican

Accommodation rather than domination had become Mussolini's preferred method of dealing with potentially influential enemies. Relations between various Italian political centers, especially Rome and the Catholic Church had a long and often confrontational history. Mussolini's own strident, youthful irreligion and the profound anti-clericalism of powerful figures in his regime, including King Victor Emmanuel III, might have led him to simply crack down on the Church and make it subservient to the government. But he preferred to reach mutually agreeable understandings that would serve both entities. In this effort he was greatly assisted by two individuals, who over three years of discussion, played important roles in reaching the desired agreements. Mussolini's brother, Arnaldo Mussolini and Eugenio Pacelli, who would become Pope Pius XII in 1939, served these crucial representations. The Concordat and other Lateran Pacts were signed on February 11, 1929. The agreements recognized the Vatican as a sovereign state and protected all properties owned by the Church in Italy, as well as assuring non-interference in Catholic education. But most importantly for Mussolini, it guaranteed that the Church would not criticize or otherwise interfere in Italian governmental matters. It brought Mussolini badly needed respect and silence about his authoritarian regime. The Treaty was later used as a model in other countries, including Germany. Pope Pius XII has been widely criticized by many historians for helping to create the pattern of passive cooperation with the Fascist and Nazi powers by surrendering the Church's moral obligations during this turbulent time. But the Church's property was protected.

Society and Culture

Fascist rule left much intact from the past. The regime did not attack the established family structure and did little to alter property ownership. It retained the constitutional monarchy, already greatly weakened before the war, and it did its best to accommodate the Catholic Church. Its "cultural revolution" was more a matter of principles and ideas than actual revolutionary changes. The dictatorship did become more radical in the 1930s but even then it left room for Italians to craft their own identities. An example of this was the retention of the annual *festa*, or days long celebrations in almost every town and village, that were so important as displays of community pride. Official public holidays mixed religious feast days with nationalistic commemorations. There was the odd sight, to our eyes, of Fascist groups parading with religious processions through the public squares.

Still, Fascist insignia and symbols were everywhere in view. Black shirts, black flags, and pretentious pictures of *Il Duce* with hints of Roman Imperial attire. Nevertheless, rival socialists and democrats were not spared the continuing raids and other intimidation on their meetings and symbols.

Rome and Milan were beginning by the 1920s to be recognized internationally as fashion centers that would soon rival Paris and New York. Fashion and design of all types, such as clothing, leather goods, architecture, interior design, and stylish automobiles were creating a major industry with significant manufacturing facilities as well as prominent marketing centers. The "Made in Italy" brand became an acknowledged mark of high quality. Milan eventually became the fashion center of Italy and a source of immense pride for Mussolini and the Fascists who took undeserved credit for this major economic development.

Musical life in Italy had long been, and remained, extremely active, but very Italian-centered and hardly international. A prominent exception was the world famous and universally admired Italian tenor, Enrico Caruso. Opera singers around the world vied for the opportunity to train and perform at the La Scala opera house in Milan, renowned as one of the best in the world. Although most of the western world was now exploring new forms of popular music, much inspired by American jazz, Italians for the most part continued to favor the great lyrical operatic treasures of Puccini, Verdi, and Mascagni. It is impossible to measure the value in economic or cultural terms of something like world leadership in a vital area of music composition and performance that existed, and continues to exist, in the field of classical opera. Whatever problems came to Italy in the 1920s, and there were many, Italians could usually find temporary solace in the hundreds of small operatic companies all over Italy.

A summation of the course of Italy in the decade of the 1920s can be expressed with two words: Mussolini and Fascism. The easy acquisition of power, the contradictions, the accommodations, and the hypocrisy all gelled together to form a totalitarian government with few restrictions or limitations. Mussolini's personal dominance was every bit as strong as Lenin's in Russia, or Kemal's in Turkey. The lessons learned from Italian Fascism were very painful for many and, hopefully, will never be repeated.

Chapter 18. Conclusion

Europe had been at war with itself, and occasionally with the United States, for centuries up to the second half of the 20th Century. But for the last sixty plus years, with the exception of civil wars and regional demands for independence, European countries have experienced unprecedented peace, and even a degree of unity. Why has this occurred and will it last? Are there reasons such as: improved and more stable economies; higher standards of living; reduced sectarian tensions in the west; greater opportunities for educational upward mobility; and far more mobile societies that broaden global perspective? Only a few decades ago, most of these questions would have been answered by many citizens of western countries with a resounding "no." Now most observers would agree that substantial progress has occurred in all of these aspects. To be sure, the progress has been uneven and subject to fits and starts, but it continues steadily at this time. So, can these positive changes of the last sixty years be traced to trends that were present and events that occurred in the 1920s? This concluding chapter will attempt to draw those connections in a logical and convincing way.

How well a country is governed is directly related to political stability and a satisfactory living standard. It is axiomatic that the more the governed are involved in the choice and operation of government, the greater will be the acceptance of policy decisions. The countries that exhibited the greatest levels of democracy, free and open press, and protection of minority rights in the 1920s were the US, Britain, France and Germany. Each had peaceful political changes through fair elections and respect for minority parties, all of which resulted in stable governments. Germany, of course, changed this direction in the 1930s, but before that, the Weimar Republic was an open and democratic government. All four of these countries experienced significant economic and social improvement during this period, and all but Germany continued this progress up to World War II. The German acceptance of a totalitarian government with its disastrous effects makes the case even stronger that political stability and long-term success depend to a great extent on popular support from an informed citizenry.

The other three countries considered here – the Soviet Union, Turkey, and Italy – either chose autocratic regimes (Turkey and Italy) or had one forced on the people (Soviet Union). There was some progress to be sure, economic growth in Italy and social modernization in Turkey, but this progress often benefited the few and was accomplished largely by force. It is hard to think of any significant governmental actions in the Soviet Union that benefitted the people. After World War II, Italy and Turkey adopted democracies that suited their countries and both have progressed reasonably well. The Soviets, however, continued the autocracy that existed before with the result that stagnation and decline in world power and prestige also continued.

Most historians have focused on the economies of a region when trying to understand and explain major movements that occur in a relatively short period of time. In attempting to explain here the impact of the economies of the selected countries on the future direction of western societies, it is best to take a macro view rather than to use labels that can be misleading. For instance, describing a national economy as, "capitalist," "socialist," or "communist," might not adequately account for the many exceptions to those general labels. Therefore, it is more useful to view an economy as one that is driven by a free and open market with limited government controls, as opposed to one that is dominated by state planning and controlled by central government management. Viewed this way, it is clear that the US, Britain, France, and Germany (in the 1920s) fit best in the former description, while the Soviet Union, Turkey and Italy match better with the latter description.

The US and Britain experienced the greatest economic development during the 1920s as their governments adopted a hands off approach to industrial and financial growth. Conservative governments in both countries were content to allow private enterprise to expand with little governmental regulation. France and Germany also promoted private sector redevelopment, but both countries had much further to go in recovery after the war that so devastated them. Impressive gains were made, however, by the end of the decade largely through low interest public funding and, eventually, private investment financing.

Italy and Turkey chose a mixed approach to guide their economic growth. Both allowed free market economies but with powerful controls from the top down. The Soviet Union was true to Marxist principles by controlling all aspects of the economy from the output of production to currency valuation. After World War I, the Soviets had the greatest economic challenges because, in addition to the destruction of major parts of their industry, there really was no significant history or experience with open market economies. A slavish adherence to communist ideology restricted almost all growth in the economy.

So by the opening of the next decade that brought global depression to everyone, the open market economies were still in better positions to persevere through to the end and recover, even though they also endured enormous human suffering.

Although the depression set back technological and scientific advances in all of the countries under review, those that started the Great War with strong and modern industries, also followed in the post-war period with far greater efficiencies and important improvements. This was especially true of the US, Britain, and Germany. Because of major damage to heavy industries in Germany, much of it done by German troops to prevent the allies from utilizing a ready resource, German industrialists were able to reconstruct their facilities using the most modern methods. By the end of the decade, German industry was on a par with the best in the industrialized world.

The major goal in every country was to transform production from human energy sources to more efficient mechanical sources. An example of this was the rapid change from the use of coal as the primary industrial energy, to the nearly universal use of electricity and oil. This was not only more efficient – fewer human hands needed in the process – but also enabled the development of modern equipment fueled by electricity and gasoline. Those countries such as the Soviet Union and Turkey that relied essentially on manpower to drive their industries lost ground in the economic race for greater productivity at lower costs. A few examples of significant changes in industrial production were the automated assembly line developed in the US, and the total process of raw materials to finished products in the ship building industry of Germany. All of the more advanced industrial societies also saw food production increase dramatically with the introduction of powerful machinery available to most farmers through government-subsidized loans.

Scientific and technological advances also played a major role in the development of military weapons and the systems to deliver them. Virtually all chronicles of national power have considered military power and economic resources as the most important aspects of a country's ability to project global power. With the exception of Germany and Italy, the rest of the countries considered here chose to significantly reduce military spending and refocus government and private spending on commercial markets. But one area of military/defense spending that did increase in the US and Britain was funding for research and development of much better aircraft, land vehicles including tanks, and naval vessels capable of delivering force all over the world.

Germany and Italy were, however, building all elements of a growing military including land forces that greatly exceeded the limits imposed by the Treaty of Versailles. The policy differences followed by these two countries were primarily based on their perception of maltreatment under the Treaty and a concern, real or exaggerated, about hostile neighbors. The Soviet Union and Turkey did not embark on significantly increased military spending until after the decade of the 1920s, primarily because of more pressing problems with their economies.

The extent to which any country or region's social and cultural activities contribute to an understanding of its international prestige and importance is difficult to measure. And in those countries where a large majority of the population is desperately poor, such as the Soviet Union and Turkey, the society's culture is not lacking in talent and desire but is too consumed with basic daily survival to attend to less urgent matters. However in France, Germany, Britain, and the US, the 1920s were rich in new ideas and directions expressed through radical movements in art, literature, music, architecture, and drama. Most of these movements were expressions of leftist ideology and total freedom from traditional restrictions. The 20s decade was unique in the first half of the century in terms of cultural freedoms and the time to express them. Before this period western societies were dominated by 19th century Victorian mores, and later decades were overwhelmed by depressions and another world war. So it is fair to say that many of the cultural and intellectual successes of the second half of the century found their origins in the 1920s. It is also true that the countries with the least democratic governments had the most repressive strictures on cultural freedom. In the Soviet Union it was governmental repression, and in Turkey and Italy it was often religious repression, Islam in Turkey and Catholicism in Italy.

Summary

To summarize the impact of the 1920s on the rest of the 20th Century in the western world, it is necessary to emphasize certain elements at the expense of others deemed to be less important. The elements considered here, at their most rudimentary levels, concern the proposition that those societies with the greatest amount of openness, freedom, and democratic governance were the ones most likely to succeed and prevail over the long term. Those governments that later chose the totalitarian system, USSR, Germany, and Italy, experienced disastrous results, whereas the open democracies have prospered and become more powerful. Of course, each nation and region has its own special challenges and the responses to those challenges do not have any universal solutions. Still, it seems obvious that the peace and stability experienced in Europe and the US at the end of the 20th Century owe much to the 1920s for the lessons learned.

BIBLIOGRAPHY

Chapter 1.

Anderson, Benedict, *Imagined Communities*. New York: Verso Books. 1991.

Cooper, Frederick and Stoler, All L (eds), *Tensions of Empire: Colonial Cultures in a Bourgeois World*. University of California, 1997.

Haugh, Richard, *The Great War at Sea 1914-1918*. Oxford University Press, 1989.

Ozment, Steven, Kagan, Donald, and Turner Frank M., *The Western Heritage*. 9th Edition, Pearson Prentice Hall, 2007.

Tuchman, Barbara, *The Guns of August*. Ballentine Books, 1962.

Chapter 2.

Ascher, Abraham, *Russia, a Short History*. New Edition, One World, 2009.

Baltzly, Alexander and Salomone, A. William, *Readings in 20th Century European History*. Appleton Century Crofts, 1950.

Fussell, Paul, *The Great War and Modern Memory*. Oxford University Press, 1989.

Garraty, John A. and Gay, Peter, *Columbia History of the World*. Harper & Row, 1981.

Haugh, Richard, *The Great War at Sea 1914-1918*. Oxford University Press, 1989.

MacMillan, Margaret, *Paris 1919*. Random House, 2002.

Chapter 3.

Bali, Rifat, *New Documents on Ataturk: Ataturk as Viewed through the Eyes of American Diplomats*. Istanbul: Isis Press, 2007.

Hanioglu, Ataturk, *An Intellectual Biography*. Princeton University Press, 2011.

Kinross, Patrick, *Ataturk: A Biography of Mustafa Kemal, Father of Modern Turkey*. New York: William Morrow, 1978.

Liggon, Helen, *The Civil War*. Wolfhound Press, 2006.

Moody, T.W. and Martin, F.X., *The Course of Irish History*. Roberts Reinhart, Revised, 2001.

Zurcher, Erik J., *Turkey: a Modern History*. I.B. Tauris & Co., 2005.

Chapter 4.

Acton, Edward, *Rethinking Russian Revolution*. Arnold, 1990.

Ascher, Abraham, *Russia: A Short History*. New Edition, One World, 2009.

Baltzly, Alexander and Salomone, A. William, *Readings in 20th Century European History*. Appleton Century Crofts, 1950.

Cornwell, John, *Hitler's Pope, the Secret Life of Pius XII*. Penquin Books, 2008.

Service, Robert, *A History of Twentieth Century Russia*. Harvard University Press, 1998.

Chapter 5.

Bosworth, R.J.B., *Mussolini*. Arnold Publishing, 2002.

Garraty, John A. and Gay, Peter, *Columbia History of the World*. Harper & Row, 1981.

Minehan, Philip, *Civil War and World War in Europe*. Palgrave Macmillan, 2011.

Overy, Richard, *1939: Countdown to War*. Penquin Books, 2011.

Ozment, Steven, Kagan, Donald, and Turner Frank M., *The Western Heritage*. 9th Edition, Pearson Prentice Hall, 2007.

Payne, Stanley G. *A History of Fascism, 1914-1945*. Univ. of Wisconsin Press, 1995.

Toland, John, *Adolf Hitler*. Anchor Books, 1992.

Chapter 6.

Atkinson, Rick, *The Day of Battle*. Henry Holt and Company, 2006.

Garraty, John A. and Gay, Peter, *Columbia History of the World*. Harper & Row, 1981.

Hastings, Max, *Inferno, the World at War 1939 – 1945*. Alfred Knopf, 2011.

Kennedy, David, *The Library of Congress, World War II Companion.* Simon & Schuster, 2007.

Olson, Lynne, *Citizens of London.* Random House, 2010.

Toye, Richard, *Churchill's Empire.* Henry Holt & Co., 2011.

Chapter 7.

Ascher, Abraham, *Russia: A Short History.* New Edition, One World, 2009.

Hitz, Frederick, *The Great Game, the Myths and Reality of Espionage.* Vintage Books, 2005.

Keep, J.L.H., *Last of the Empires: A History of the Soviet Union, 1945-1991.* Oxford, 1995.

Ozment, Steven, Kagan, Donald, and Turner Frank M., *The Western Heritage.* 9th Edition, Pearson Prentice Hall, 2007.

Panayi, P. and Lareres, K. Eds., *The Federal Republic of Germany since 1949: Politics, Society and Economy before and after Unification.* London, Longman, 1996.

Service, Robert, *A History of Twentieth Century Russia.* Harvard University Press, 1998.

Chapter 8.

Drake, Richard, *The Soviet Dimension of Italian Communism, Journal of Cold War Studies.* 2004.

Gilberg, Troad, *Coalition Strategies of Marxist Parties.* Duke University Press, 1989.

Kertzer, David, *Parties and Symbols, The Italian Communist Party and the Fall of Communism.* Yale University Press, 1998.

Minehan, Philip, *Civil War and World War in Europe.* Palgrave Macmillan, 2011.

Thomas, Martin, *The French Empire Between the Wars.* Manchester University Press, 2005.

Chapter 9.

Ascher, Abraham, *Russia: A Short History.* New Edition, One World, 2009.

Brown, A., *The Gorbachev Factor*. Oxford, 1997.

Garton Ash, Timothy, *The Polish Revolution, Solidarity*. Yale University Press, 2002.

Service, Robert, *A History of Twentieth Century Russia*. Harvard University Press, 1998.

Shatz, M.S., *Soviet Dissent in Historical Perspective*. New York, 1980.

Chapter 10.

Kuisel, Richard, *Seducing the French: The Dilemma of Americanization*. University of California Press, 1997.

Laqueur, Walter, *The Last Days of Europe, Epitaph for an Old Continent*. St. Martin's Press, 2007.

Samuelson, Robert, *The End of Europe*. Washington Post, June 15, 2005.

Chapter 11.

Goldberg, Ronald, *America in the Twenties*. Syracuse University Press, 2003.

Hawley, Ellis, *The Great War and the Search for a Modern Order*. St. Martin's Press, 1992.

Palmer, Niall, *The Twenties in America*. Edinburgh University Press, 2006.

Plesur, Milton, *The 1920s Problems and Paradoxes*. Allyn and Bacon, Inc., 1969.

Schlesinger, Jr., Arthur, *The Crisis of the Old Order*. Houghton Mifflin Company, 1957.

Chapter 12.

Ascher, Abraham, *Russia: a Short History*. New Edition, One World, 2009.

Chambers, Frank, Phelps Harris, Christina, and Bayley, Charles, *This Age of Conflict*. Harcourt, Brace and Company, 1950.

Scheffer, Paul, *Seven Years in Soviet Russia*. Hyperian Press, 1931.

Service, Robert, *A History of Twentieth Century Russia*. Harvard University Press, 1998.

Treadgold, Donald, *Twentieth Century Russia.* Rand McNally & Company, 1959.

Chapter 13.

Carr, William, *A History of Germany 1815 – 1945.* St. Martin's Press, 1969.

Dorpalen, Andreas, *Hindenburg and the Weimar Republic.* Princeton University Press, 1964.

Friedrich, Otto, *Before the Deluge, a Portrait of Berlin in the 1920s.* Harper Collins Publishers, 1995.

Jacobson, Jon, *Locarno Diplomacy, Germany and the West.* Princeton University Press, 1972.

Taylor, Frederick, *The Downfall of Money.* Bloomsbury Press, 2013.

Chapter 14.

Blake, Robert, *The Decline of Power.* Oxford University Press, 1985.

Mowat, Charles, *Britain Between the Wars 1918 – 1940.* University of Chicago Press, 1955.

Overy, Richard, *The Twilight Years.* Viking, 2009.

Spector, Ronald, *At War At Sea.* Viking 2001.

Toye, Richard, *Churchill's Empire.* Henry Holt and Company, 2010.

Wilson, Trevor, *The Downfall of the Liberal Party 1914 – 1935.* Cornell University Press, 1966.

Chapter 15.

Hanioglu, M. Sukru, *Ataturk, an Intellectual Biography.* Princeton University Press, 2011.

Price, M. Philips, *A History of Turkey from Empire to Republic.* Humanities Press, Inc., 1968.

Vali, Ferenc A., *Bridge Across the Bosporus.* Johns Hopkins Press, 1971.

Chapter 16.

Chambers, Frank, Phelps Harris, Christina, and Bayley, Charles, *This Age of Conflict.* Harcourt, Brace and Company, 1950.

de Sauvigny, G. de Bertier and Pinkney, David, *History of France.* The Forum Press, 1977.

Knapton, Ernest John, *France Since Versailles.* Holt, Rinehart and Winston, 2003.

Thomas, Martin, *The French Empire Between the Wars.* Manchester University Press, 2005.

Chapter 17.

Bosworth, R.J.B., *Mussolini's Italy, Life under the Dictatorship 1915 – 1945.* The Penguin Press, 2006.

Duggan, Christopher, *Fascist Voices: an Intimate History of Mussolini's Italy.* Oxford University Press, 2013.

Finaldi, Guiseppe, *Mussolini and Italian Fascism.* Pearson Education Limited, 2008.

Gregor, A. James, *Italian Fascism and Development Dictatorship.* Princeton University Press, 1979.

Salvemini, Gaetano, *The Fascist Dictatorship in Italy.* Howard Fertig, 1967.

Salvemini, Gaetano, T*he Origins of Fascism in Italy.* Harper & Row Publishers, 1973.

Schneider, Herbert, *Making the Fascist State,* Oxford University Press, 1968.

INDEX